DREAMING WIT

DREAMING
WITH
TONY DE MELLO

A HANDBOOK OF MEDITATION EXERCISES

JOHN CALLANAN, SJ

MERCIER PRESS

MERCIER PRESS
PO Box 5, 5 French Church Street, Cork
   and
16 Hume Street, Dublin

Trade enquiries to CMD DISTRIBUTION,
55a Spruce Avenue, Stillorgan Industrial Park, Blackrock, Dublin

ISBN 1 85635 192 0
A CIP record for this book is available from the British Library.

10 9 8 7 6 5 4 3

DEDICATION

To all those who were trusting and honest enough to share with me their
innermost beings and their experience of the Mystery we call God.

Printed in Ireland by Colour Books Ltd.

CONTENTS

Acknowledgements

This book has been written with the encouragement of many people. I would like to thank especially my family for their constant support and my community for their patience. Particular thanks must go to my brother Bill Callanan, SJ, for his illustrations as well as to Eddie O'Donnell, SJ, and Donal Neary, SJ, for their unfailing help. Also to the Wynne family for their support and assistance. I remember with gratitude those who suggested topics and ideas for some of the meditations and fantasy exercises. In some instances I have borrowed concepts or outlines without being sure of their authorship and I crave forgiveness of those whose materials I dipped into. Finally, many people on retreats and workshops have told me what goes on for them during their meditations and prayer time and insofar as this has shaped the final form of the exercises I cannot express my gratitude to them deeply enough.

INDEX OF MEDITATIONS AND FANTASY EXERCISES

INTRODUCTION

Since my first book on Fr Tony de Mello came out a number of people have asked me to put together further thoughts about the man and his message. They say they have been inspired by him. So let's start with the basic details.

Born in Bombay in 1931 Fr Tony de Mello was an Indian Jesuit who had a profound influence on those who met him. Biographical details are scarce enough and hard to find but he himself has said that his early faith and enthusiasm for Christianity were most probably given to him during his earliest childhood experiences in India. During those early years he was exposed to both Hindu and Buddhist traditions, which intermingled with his simple Christianity.

Tony de Mello joined the Society of Jesus in 1947, before his sixteenth birthday, and whilst still a young Jesuit he was sent by his superiors to Spain, so that he might study spirituality. In that country he was profoundly influenced by a number of Spanish saints and Christian mystical writers – most notably Teresa of Avila and John of the Cross. Subsequently he was sent by his Jesuit superiors to the United States to study psychology. A number of observers have noted that the fusion of De Mello's psychological background – which dealt with the strengths and weaknesses of human nature – coupled with reflections upon the theories of good and evil contained in both eastern and western spirituality, provided him with the explosive mixture which he afterwards used with his students.

During the latter part of his life, Tony de Mello ran courses and workshops in the Sadhana Retreat Centre near Bombay, as well as conducting seminars and prayer workshops around the world. He died suddenly in New York in June 1987 while conducting such a workshop at Fordham University.

Since his death his star has continued to shine. Many say it has even brightened. More and more people seem to find inspiration in his words and spirit. I can personally vouch for the fact that Tony de Mello was an explosive teacher and speaker in the spiritual sphere. He had the rare gift of bringing vitality and spiritual energy wherever he went. This was never more evident to me than on his first visit to Ireland in 1977. Tony de Mello had made a huge impact on the 32nd General Congregation of the Jesuits in Rome and, possibly, because of this the Irish Jesuit Provincial invited him to address a local group of priests, brothers and students in a retreat house in the Irish midlands. Almost as soon as he arrived, you could sense the electricity in the air. Everything he touched had a fresh feel about it and the spirit he managed to produce on that first evening was astounding – at least to me. Straight away, his listeners were challenged to their very cores, for much of what he said made them directly question what they had been brought up to believe. Years of seminary training took a severe jolt – or so it seemed to me at the time. Many spent the entire evening spellbound. What De Mello spoke about was at once both refreshing and frightening. It left a thirst for life that remains within many of his listeners to this very day. Whereas some disagreed with what he had to say, I think very few were unmoved. I hope you will not be either as you work your way through the exercises and meditations contained in this book. They are based and modelled on the style used by De Mello.

May his spirit continue to challenge and encourage us.

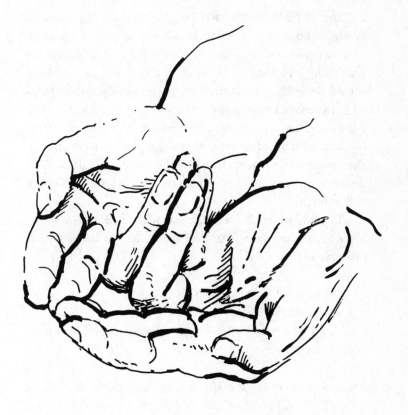

Mudras are used in Tantric meditation as an energy-channelling device.

BEGINNINGS

Nothing is true or untrue but thinking makes it so.

WILLIAM SHAKESPEARE

Fr Tony de Mello was something of a guru, an inspiration, a beacon of hope and a fountain of wisdom as well as a purveyor of new life to many. Since his death, both his work and the spirituality he attempted to encourage in others seem to have spread like wildfire. Few can doubt that he had a gift which helped faith come alive for those who came into contact with him. Perhaps he had a particular relevance for faith life today insofar as he both dared and was capable of placing in perspective the institutional element of Christianity and thus he allowed his audience the chance to both search for and find the Christ alive within them.

To many who will not be familiar with Fr Tony de Mello or his work the questions that will spring to mind readily will probably be:

- Who was this Tony de Mello?
- What did he teach?
- And why have his teachings and spirit gained such popularity?

As mentioned in the introduction, Fr Tony de Mello was an Indian Jesuit who had a profound influence on those who met him. It's evident now in retrospect that De Mello touched and radically altered the lives of many – but how did he do that? Some, at least, of what he taught must have been both profound and of lasting value. Any who were lucky enough to personally have been participants on his spirituality courses in Sadhana, India, or on his workshops or retreats on prayer and spirituality throughout the world will attest to the fact that the very manner and enthusiasm with which he spoke added greatly to, and sharpened, his message. During those retreats he never flagged and constantly seemed to both enjoy and gain energy from what he taught. One who did attend such gatherings said of him, 'he was a touchingly loving man – one who could gauge the strengths and limits of others, who could affirm as well as point out gentle lifestyle warnings with a detached air – one who left his listeners free, left them with a sense of daring, and left them with the ability to question and not accept everything at face value, nor accept it uncritically, just because it was spoken by a figure of authority. He was a man who was capable of helping people break free, one who helped those he encountered fight the oppressor within each of us'.

So what was Tony de Mello like as a teacher and guide? To say he was a teacher in the conventional sense of the word may well be inaccurate. Rather, he seemed to have the facility to open up for people their inner selves to themselves, in a way that was challenging, encouraging and insightful. It could also be both frightening and fun as many who attended his retreats and seminars will affirm. I have asked various individuals what Tony de Mello's workshops, books or tapes have meant to them and have received a plethora of replies. Some stress the concept of self-awareness – the ability to look critically at what's going on in one's own life – and this indeed was a golden web running through De Mello's spirituality. Others who knew Tony de Mello personally cite the store of encouragement and life-giving zest which he instilled in their lives. He had that rare gift of bringing life wherever he went. His stories went right to the heart of matters, and to the hearts of his listeners. He managed to make Christ real and alive for people. As Christ gave living faith and courage to his listeners so De Mello instilled in his retreat audiences the fact that there were potential golden eagles among them. At the De Mello workshops and retreats I attended myself, it soon became clear that some of us were unaware of the heights to which we could soar and to me this is another of De Mello's insights – he encouraged in all he met fulfilment of their potential. Tony often mentioned the fact that most human beings function at about 2% of their potential. If this statement scares you a little then I know it also scares the devil out of me. He pointed out that we go through our lives almost in a state of sleep and highlighted the danger that we may never waken up, never realise that we are asleep and thus we may never do anything about realising our potential.

Tony de Mello was a liberator. He blessed and cherished religion and yet warned of its perils. He asked us to keep an eye on the commonly held beliefs of society as well as keeping our gaze on institutionalised religion lest it constrain or maim us. In his workshops and retreats he constantly recommended that we take our religious beliefs and test them as gold is tested in the fire, finding out what beliefs stand up to the harsh realities of 'day to day' faith living and which were base metal that would ultimately be found wanting and fail us in the real life of the spirit. That was what his work was about – waking people up to the reality of their greatness and letting them know how great God believed them to be.

At his best, Tony de Mello proclaimed the message of awareness, brilliantly. He helped individuals with whom he came into contact recognise that they were better than they themselves were prepared to believe. To him, true spirituality meant waking up – though he doubted the capacity of many to change. 'As I grow older,' he said, 'I become resigned to the fact that people are the way they are, and one might as well accept the fact and learn to live with it. I think most of our troubles with people come from our demanding, or expecting, or hoping that they will change. Normally, they do not. They are born asleep, they live asleep and they die in their sleep without ever waking up. Thus they never really understand the beauty and the excitement of life'.

Refusing to act on one's potential is a sort of illness. Tony de Mello constantly pointed to Christ as a model – one who was true to his own inner promptings and who relentlessly followed his inner voice. We should do the same. 'The responsibility,' he said, 'for your growth is on your own shoulders'. Then he added a rider: 'Most people don't really want to be cured of self-doubt and failure. They don't want to be a success and neither do they want to reach their full potential. Why? Because the cost involved is too high'.

De Mello said, 'A teacher teaches, but a guru guides an individual to discover self, God, and reality'. We need gurus today, people who have experienced God themselves and who feel secure enough to guide others to mysticism. He believed that there is a place for mysticism in all our lives. The best way for me to try to explain what he meant is to present some De Mello-like exercises straight away. Let me begin with an easy one.

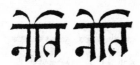

Neti Neti: These two Sandscrit words mean 'Not this: not that', and are used to remind the pupil not to take appearances for reality.

A MEDITATION ON MY OWN BREATH

Quieten yourself ...

Settle into a balanced comfortable position ...

Take a slow and deep breath ... count slowly up to four as you take each breath in and let each breath out.

Let out the breath with a deep sigh.

Continue with these deep and slow breaths for a couple of minutes ...

Just be quiet ... feel the calmness ... hear the silence ... sense the natural rhythm.

Concentrate on what is happening while you breath: notice that the air is coldish coming in through your nostrils, warmer on its way out ...

Now relax completely and let your breath flow easily ... without effort ...

Just be aware of your natural breathing.

Whenever your mind wanders, take note of the wandering and return to an awareness of your breath pattern.

When you have spent some little time on this exercise, bring yourself back to the present place and time.

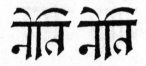

RELEASING TENSION

Move slowly through the different parts of your body, beginning with the forehead. Lightly tense your forehead, hold that tension for a moment, then release the tension. Now move to the eyes, mouth, neck, shoulders, chest, stomach, buttocks, legs and feet. Lightly tense each part in turn, holding for two or three seconds, and then release the tension and stay with that feeling for a short while. Once you have moved around your whole body you should feel very relaxed. Let your mind and body join in letting go of all the tension. Feel the stillness within you and after some little time stretch your body slowly and finish the exercise.

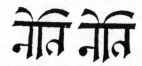

MEDITATION ON A SEA SHORE

Use one of the suggested preparatory exercises.

In your imagination place yourself alone on a sea shore. Allow your mind to think about the many aspects of your life that have grown far too big and out of proportion during the past year. Search for these phoney big things. When you have discovered aspects of yourself that you would like to be less time-consuming, go on to see if there are aspects of life that you are neglecting. How will you make time for these elements?

Give yourself time, space and solitude.

As a second part to this fantasy exercise and if it is not too threatening, you might like to imagine yourself in your grave. Look at present decisions you are making from that viewpoint.

It puts things into perspective!

Anajali Mudra: 'I bow to the light within you'.
The Namaskar, or traditional Indian greeting; both hands are raised to the level of the chest to greet equals, to the forehead when coming into the presence of a revered person or God.

GETTING STARTED

The object of meditation is to transform oneself, not to have good meditations.

SANGHARAKSHITA

Now we need to look at hints that may help us to pray. As Cardinal Basil Hume has said, if people only prayed when they felt like it they would hardly pray at all. So can we draw upon basic principles and practices that may assist us? These pages are an attempt to do just that. They are, in a sense, very basic hints aimed at those who are working with small prayer groups, but they should be equally helpful to those attempting to pray on their own. In recent years I have spent quite a lot of time working with adult and youth groups on prayerful fantasy exercises, gospel meditations and quieting exercises. These people have asked me to set down, in not too grand a fashion, how one might pray today. They ask:

- Can I pray?
- Do I want to pray?
- How can I find the time to pray?
- Where should I pray?
- In what way does one pray?
- What will help me as I pray?
- How best might I facilitate groups to pray?

In an attempt to answer these questions here are some basic hints.

FIND A PLACE

Finding a place is your first task. What you need is a location that is reasonably quiet and not too cold, where both yourself and the participants feel fairly safe. It helps to have carpet on the floor along with a number of straight-backed chairs. A number of cushions would also help. I also use and recommend a lighting system that can be dimmed to add atmosphere to the room and to this I add candles, both for devotional and atmospheric purposes. I normally place a large Taize-style cross in the room as well, to remind myself of what I am about. Lest all this sounds very expensive or out of your reach, I should say that a school of my acquaintance produced just such a prayer centre and set the whole operation up, from a barren shell, for just a few hundred pounds though I do admit they had to beg, borrow and wheeler-deal to achieve this. It may be a good idea to use, where possible, the same place each day as the area chosen will gradually take on an aura of spiritual quietness.

FIND A TIME

Any time is suitable, really, though some time-slots are more helpful than others. Many find that it is useful, where possible, to ensure that the daily prayer period takes place at the beginning of the day because at the end of a long day's happenings, the mind is in a state of flux, whereas in the morning it is relatively quiet. It is useful to have some idea of your own body-clock. You thus know what time suits you best for prayer. When working with groups, the individual members will often be able to tell you what time suits them best. Certainly their demeanour will let you know if the hour you have chosen is a wildly unsuitable one for them.

GETTING THE SESSION STARTED

Perhaps the key moments are the first ones. There's much to be done. Group members have to be settled and focused. This is particularly true where younger group members are involved. You need to take time so that the participants' prayer can settle. I have included at the end of each chapter numerous introductory exercises which you can use either for yourself or whilst working with a group.

I normally begin by lighting a candle and then darken the room. I often use background music by playing one of the reflective meditation tapes. I then talk slowly with the participants asking them to focus upon the task ahead and to place themselves in God's presence. I continue talking both quietly and slowly, asking them to do their best to be aware of what they are attempting to do and I often ask them to concentrate and become aware of their pattern of breathing. This slow and quiet introduction usually begins to settle the group after a short time. If it doesn't, I know I'm in big trouble and, I may spend the time talking to them rather than attempting a meditation or prayer exercise which I know has little chance of succeeding. Better to come back when the ground may be more fertile than to abort in mid-stride. If the group is moderately unsettled, I may well continue to talk slowly and quietly, bringing the group members bit by bit into a more serene and reflective state where, hopefully, they may find God or be found by Him. I cannot stress too strongly here that getting the group settled is, for me, of paramount importance if anything useful and prayerful is going to happen and I spend whatever amount of time is necessary in an attempt to achieve the right atmosphere. I have occasionally been known to spend three-quarters of the allotted time settling the group and then I use whatever period remains on the prayer itself rather than begin too hastily. If the group is not settled you have, in my view, little or no chance of having a successful meditation.

A nice story illustrates this point which for me is a key one. I recall a famous lion-tamer whose most fabulous trick was putting his head into a lion's mouth each evening during a circus performance. He was asked on a radio show – when he retired and was still in good health – how he had been so successful. Well, he said, 'each evening when I made my way into the lion's cage I talked quietly to the audience who had come to watch the show, but in reality my task during this time was to work with my favourite lioness, Betsy – the one into whose mouth I would later place my head – in the hope of gauging the temperature or the humour of the animals in the group. I did this by patting my lioness first on the rump as I made my opening comments to the crowd. My lioness always growled. A couple of moments further into my act I patted Betsy along her side and she growled again. Still later, I patted her on the head and listened for her final growl. Depending on the vibes I picked up from her growls, I decided whether or not to place my head in her mouth that evening. That's how I kept my head'.

I could say something similar when it comes to preparing prayer and fantasy sessions with young people. The first few minutes are spent testing the atmosphere and humour of the group. Upon that depends how deeply you will attempt to go into prayer with the group.

BREATH CONTROL

Tony de Mello used to say that, in eastern-style prayer, your breath is your greatest friend. I usually take a little time to describe how the participants might become aware and control the pace of their breathing. Building up a nice steady pace of breathing helps to settle us. You can be helped here by imagining that you are breathing the light from a candle in and out. If you have a candle, place it in the centre of the group. Then almost close your eyes and you will see sparks of golden light jetting out from the candle flame. Imagine these are the light of the spirit and thus breathe the spirit in and out. I suggest counting inwardly as you breathe in and out at the beginning of the session and it will help with the breathing rhythm. Keeping your lips closed, you imagine the air coming in through your nostrils to the back of your throat, down into your shoulders, down your arms, circling around your backbone and thence down to the very pit of your stomach. As you breathe in, you imagine you are taking in the peace of Christ, or the harmony you require in your life, and as your breathe out, you visualise yourself letting go of all the tensions, frustrations, anger and aggression that may have built up during the period since your last meditation. Be mindful, but don't force your mind. If it wanders, gently bring it back to being mindful of your breath pattern again. Be patient.

A second exercise that helps you to focus is to imagine in your mind that you are starting the prayer session on the ground floor of a building. In your imagination, you begin to travel down to the basement. You imagine that your are going down stairs, slowly, each step at a time, until you get to a place deep within you where you can talk to your God. If you use this procedure, you should remember to bring the group members back up the stairs slowly at the end of the session so that they can return peacefully to the here and now.

DISTRACTIONS
No matter what type of prayer you are engaged in, you will probably find that distractions of various kinds invade your space. When you notice these occurring, you simply note them and then come back to where you are in the meditation. We cannot avoid having distractions, nor can we fight them, so if they come, let them, and having become aware of them, allow them go away again. It may help to say something like the following to yourself: 'Don't interrupt me now, I will attend to you later', and keep this appointment because the distractions may in fact be trying to tell you something about yourself.

In the west generally, people do not pay much attention to their breath control but in the east they do. They know that our breathing can be related to our physical well-being. When we are stressed and tense our breathing becomes erratic, gasping, shallow, panting and so on. Our body knows our state of mind. Our spirit knows it also. Our breathing may be shallow or deep, fast or slow. Just note which is the case for you. Also, close your eyes. In prayer, we are trying to quieten the mind, which is a bit like a pool, whose surface, when ruffled by the winds of anger or confusion is unable to reflect the sun. Shutting the eyes may also shut out distractions. While we are practising meditation, we are engaged in a mental effort which requires some simple physical support. It is not unusual to be distracted by aches and pains in the back or the legs. What we need to find is a position which allows the body to be completely at ease for as long as we wish. Take up a position which keeps the head and spine erect, the whole body at once both poised and alert, yet relaxed and comfortable. Your chair should be straight-backed so that the vertebrae of your back sit one on top of the other. Younger people will sometimes opt for a slouched position, thinking it is more comfortable. In the long run it is not. Nor is an easy chair, despite its obvious attractions. I normally show group members a simple prayer-stool and explain that its function is to help the person praying take up a posture that is both comfortable and focused. As the prayer-stool keeps the back straight, it also helps to regularise the breathing.

LYING DOWN

I hesitate to suggest this posture whilst working with groups unless the group is both settled and mature. If members wish to try this prayer position, they may need to bring a cushion and rug with them. Then, lying on the floor, they use the cushion to lay their head on and may wish to use the rug to lie on or to cover themselves if the temperature is chilly. They keep their legs straight, not crossed, and hold their arms by their sides.

This prayer position is great, but has one slight disadvantage which is readily apparent. One runs the great risk of falling asleep. To counter this, a friend of mine worked out a system whereby he held his two arms straight up in the air as he lay on the ground and found that if he began to get sleepy both of his arms would begin to fall to the floor and in that way, he would be awakened before unwanted sleep overcame him.

THE YOGA POSITION

In Indian ashrams or prayer centres the ideal posture for prayer is normally thought to be a 'full lotus' sitting position. In fact any bodily posture which assists a higher state of consciousness is known by the traditional eastern term 'mudra' but the 'full lotus' position consists of seven aspects which a wise Indian lady told me Europeans could not manage without doing serious injury to themselves. 'We are trained to it since birth,' she explained. 'Why not try the "half-lotus" instead?' To try this you need a cushion which is fairly firm and you seat yourself on this against a wall. Your legs should be crossed with each foot placed, sole uppermost, upon the thigh of the other leg and your spine should be straight and upright. Usually you hold the hands in the lap, your palms both facing upward, one over the other so that the thumb-tips lightly touch. Keep your shoulders relaxed and your eyes closed or slightly open.

LISTENING

We spend much of our time, consciously or subconsciously, listening. We listen to friends, to members of our families, to our colleagues and associates, to the people we meet in our daily work, or to those we meet in shops or on the street. Even in our leisure hours we tune in to radio or television programmes with a listening ear and are constantly alive to the muted sounds of our background environment. Through this listening, we have all developed skills. We pick out different people's voices, their attitudes and emotions, their openness and honesty. We have learned how to extract useful information from listening and know how to relate this information to ourselves. In the meditations described below we listen again – to the gentle spirit which whispers within us, to our bodies and humours perhaps yelling at us, and to the voice of our God trying to make itself heard amongst the noise.

An ancient Chinese proverb tells us that the hardest part of a journey is the first step, just taking the risk to set out. As with any fearsome journey, there are a hundred reasons why you should be aware of taking on the challenge, but, as one vastly experienced travel writer has said, in the final analysis, the best advice if you want to live is, 'just go'.

CHRIST BEFORE ME

In this exercise you first settle yourself and become aware of your breathing. Then close your eyes. Some people have great difficulty doing this and have to be gently reminded during the prayer time to keep their eyes closed or only slightly open in order to avoid unnecessary distractions. Now imagine Christ standing in front of you and speaking personally to you. Take your time and let Christ's words come slowly. You may feel both love and pain, as though He understood you more than you ever gave Him credit for. It may be a healing experience. Through your tears you may feel the release of a certain amount of tension.

THE WOMAN AT THE WELL
(John 4:5–30)

Read the gospel passage.

Start by settling yourself and placing yourself in God's presence. Now fill the body with air to its maximum capacity and then try to empty it as far as possible. Begin to breath, slowly and deeply, with lips closed, both inhaling and exhaling through the nose. Count the breaths, thinking of nothing save the counting. Now use the imagination. Active imagination allows the self to participate dynamically in the dialogue between the conscious and the unconscious within ourselves. Imagine yourself in the countryside on a summer day. As you walk along, you notice a large well and as the day is warm and you are thirsty, you begin to drink. Now sit under the shade of a nearby tree and in your imagination see Jesus, tired from his day's work, come close to the well. Now note the woman coming with a bucket to draw water for her daily needs. Watch as Jesus begins to talk to her. Her natural response may be to turn away in fear or distrust. However, dialogue starts and the ice is broken. The woman listens and her heart begins to open. She asks for some of this life-giving water. Take some time and allow Jesus to come to you. Listen to what he says to you in your imagination. What does he ask of you? What is your response? Now change your attention and go back in your mind to the day of your baptism. As the priest pours water over your forehead, feel the cool water and experience the life-giving spirit and the healing forgiveness of the Father filling your whole being. Take some time and experience the different feelings within you right now. Take some time with Jesus and share your feelings with him.

First read the passage in St John's gospel.

Quieten yourself in the usual way and become aware of any sounds you can hear outside the room. After a little time, allow your attention to come inwards and note what sounds you can hear within the room. Finally, draw your attention further inwards and see if you can notice any sounds within yourself. You may be able to hear the sound of air as it comes quietly through your nostrils. Note your breathing for this will help you to attain silence. God's revealing word is often best received in silence. Having read about the woman at the well in St John's gospel, you pause at the places where something in the script touches you. You might notice that Jesus talks to the woman and asks something of her. She wonders why He is talking to her for it is not usual in her society. She knows she is an outcast and thinks she can do little about her circumstances. Christ thinks differently. We are working on two levels here. The woman is being offered an opportunity to get in touch with her deeper desires. So are we. Slowly reflect on the fact that Christ may also be talking to me. He may be helping me get in touch with my deepest desires. Am I being offered the living water? If so, where might it be found by me?

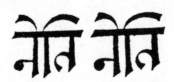

The Matayoni Mudra
A gesture of reverence associated with the Mother-goddess.

OBSERVING YOURSELF

He has half the deed done, who has made a beginning.

There's a very small village high up in the north of Zambia which I visited some months ago and a number of the locals told me a story which is well know in their hamlet. They said they had a simple lad in the village called Simon and when he reached the age of eighteen he decided to take himself off to the capital city, Lusaka, as he was a bit tired of village life, and anyway he wanted to make his way in the world as well as make his fortune. And so he set out and reached the capital. All that first day he trudged about, looking for employment and the beginnings of his new life, but by the time that first evening arrived, he found himself no better off than when he had reached the city and thus he decided that it might be wise to find himself shelter for the night. This operation didn't prove too easy as accommodation was both scarce and expensive, and Simon had little enough money to spend. He finally decided to follow the crowds he saw wandering around as he felt sure they must be heading for some place of frugal rest. At length, most of them ended up in the forecourt of the main railway station where they settled down to sleep for the evening, either individually or in groups. Poor Simon decided he better do the same but being a simple boy from the country, and never having seen such crowds before, he was completely bemused by the huge teeming masses of humanity who were settling down around him. 'With so many people jumbled up together for the night,' Simon said to himself, 'and with their arms and legs so intertwined together, how will I ever be able to find myself when I wake up in the morning?' Then, being a simple fellow, he had an idea. He had in his pocket a balloon which he took out and blew up, and then with a bit of string tied it to his leg reasoning that when he woke up in the morning all he had to do was look in the air and wherever he saw the balloon he'd know that he himself was attached to it. And that is what he did. He tied the balloon to one ankle and went to sleep happily, content in the knowledge that when he awoke he only had to search for the balloon in the air to rediscover where he himself was.

Unfortunately for him, there was in the station forecourt a practical joker who had noticed the whole performance and thought he would have a bit of fun at the simple lad's expense. As soon as Simon was asleep, the practical joker went over and untied the balloon from Simon's leg and going over to a far corner of the station the joker retied the balloon to his own leg so that when Simon awoke in the morning he looked first in his own vicinity but could discover nothing. After some time he noticed the balloon flying gaily on the other side of the station hall and he said to himself, 'If I can't even find myself I am in big trouble'.

This story illustrates nicely enough one of the purposes of prayer. We are trying to talk to and listen to God, to observe ourselves and thus attempt to see ourselves as God sees us. In the sort of prayer Tony de Mello illustrated, we try to be honest about who we are, where we are going, and do our best to be more aware of how we relate to ourselves, to those around us, and to our God. These traits are particularly apparent in the fantasy exercises De Mello was so fond of employing. Using fantasy as a form of prayer is quite novel to us in the west but was more common to De Mello with his eastern background. Many adults, and particularly young people, are greatly helped today by this form of prayer. At least the ones I am in contact with are.

A brief story may illustrate one way in which fantasy-style meditations may help us. When I was a small child, we had a pleasant river running quite near our house. My brothers and sisters and I sometimes used to make excursions there to fish for pinkeens or minnows. The process we used was as follows. We would carry with us large empty jam-jars and as soon as we got to the river bank we tied a large hoop of twine around the necks of the jam-jars. Then very carefully we lowered their necks into the water and tipped them on their sides, leaving the mouths of the jars exposed. The tiny fish, being shy but curious creatures by nature, would slowly circle around the mouths of the jars. They never actually swam into the jars themselves but they were often tempted to poke their noses around the rim and inspect this new article which had come into their domain. That was the moment we were waiting for. Judging the moment to perfection, we had to snatch the jam-jar rapidly out of the water by means of the string attached to the jar's neck and when we finally got the jar into our hands, it was full of very murky and muddy water. Even by holding it up to the light, you could not really see if you had caught anything worthwhile or not. Our next task was to walk home carefully with the jam-jars full of their murky contents. Having left the jam-jars and their muddy contents to settle overnight we would get up in the morning and find that – while we slept – great things had been happening. Muddy water, if it is allowed to settle, becomes still and then begins to clear. So it was with our jars. Because we had allowed things to settle overnight, the muddy water had filtered itself and we could now see clearly whether it contained any worthwhile life or not.

Fantasy prayer can have a somewhat similar effect upon us. Most of us are so busy and rushed off our feet that we never give ourselves time to settle and thus find it very difficult to find out what elements are truly important in our lives. The gift fantasy-style prayer may give us is an opportunity to take time out, to settle ourselves, to let our inner selves become still and then – in the stillness – Christ may reveal himself to us. As Kafka says, 'I have an inescapable duty to observe myself. If someone else is observing me, naturally I have to observe myself too. If no one else observes me, I have to observe myself all the closer'. St Ignatius, in his autobiography, said something similar. He explained that he regularly needed to take time out just to be still and to reflect on what was going on in his life. He considered this to be a vital exercise and claimed that he had been given a great blessing by God when, having been injured in a battle fairly early on in life, he was forced to rest and recuperate from his injuries. During this time of resting, he found that by looking back and dwelling on what had gone on in his life during the recent past, he could discern what areas of his life were bearing fruit and which were barren. 'Go back to where you have found fruit', he would say. In other words, finding time for reflection allows us to discover where the finger of God has been tracing itself in our lives during the past months. When we know this we may be able to see where we should devote more time and energy if we wish to encounter Christ more readily in the future. The idea of taking time out and 'just being' quiet with the Lord is not a new one, of course. Many spiritual masters recommend it. They advise us to take the time just to sit, to be silent, doing little more than looking and listening to the Lord. This, I regret to say, is a good deal easier said than done. Tony de Mello taught us that in many Buddhist centres, the adherents spent a good deal of time just sitting and looking. He said that when he himself took time out in such establishments he was counselled to just sit and look at the birds, or the trees, or the beauty of nature. Having spent some time in a Buddhist ashram in India myself, I found I was somewhat similarly advised. Much the same thing happened a few years ago when I went on retreat to a Franciscan house of prayer. I intended making an eight-day silent retreat and asked a Franciscan retreat director to guide me. For the first day or two he advised me to just rest and relax – in short to 'just be'. I expected to be given pieces of scripture to reflect on but days One and Two contained none such. When I made my daily visit to my retreat director on day Three, the wise man asked me to go cliff-walking and see if I could discover any birds nesting as we were then in the breeding season. This advice was followed on day Four with the suggestion that I should sit on the cliff-tops and really notice the colours of the sea. Day Five was taken up with somewhat similar counsel. I was to sit on a rock and see how cloud formations made their way across the sky. By this stage I was really desperate. I pleaded for some scripture to work with but the director wasn't really keen. He only allowed formal prayer after much persuasion. He had, as I understand it, been more alive to the prompting of the spirit than I was myself. He had seen how I could busy myself with all sorts of scriptural paraphernalia and never really encounter the Lord. In my busyness, I might prevent the Lord from ever having the opportunity of encountering or communicating with me.

Scott Peck, the famous American author, has said that he spends two hours every day just doing nothing and spiritual writers down through the ages have reiterated much the same thing. Anselm, a spiritual giant who lived between 1033 and 1109 laid stress on much the same point:

> And rest aside in Him
> Enter the inner chamber of your soul
> Shut out everything except God
> And that which can help you in seeking Him
> Now, my whole heart, say to God,
> I seek your face,
> Lord, it is your face I seek.

St Augustine, perhaps a more famous early Christian writer, preached a similar message. He advised his listeners to adhere to the following dictum: 'Make sure your life sings the same tune as your mouth'. He means that your life might be the only book another person reads and you cannot be sure that both your life and your mouth are in harmony unless you take time out to reflect on what's going on within you. In fact, if you do not take the necessary time for such reflection, there may be considerable disharmony between what you say and what you do. Fr Bill Johnston, an Irish Jesuit who has worked for many years in Japan, regularly points out that in the east they place great store in finding self-reflection time. A popular saying there is, 'sit down, be quiet and be at peace'.

In this book many fantasy exercises and gospel meditations are set out. Don't rush through them. Give yourself time to work with them and remember that if you want to see the fruits of your meditation, then St Augustine's remarks about making your life sing the same song as your mouth may not cause you embarrassment. Take the time to look at your life and at your relationships. Hopefully they will be in harmony.

This practice of self-observation and finding out where the finger of God has been tracing itself in one's life may be painful at times. Let me give an example. I know that every year one of the days that I look forward to most excitedly is the day of the English Football Cup Final. I prepare for the event with great diligence. Right at the beginning of the year I put a big mark in my diary against that date to make certain that I won't miss the event. When the day itself arrives I have left myself free and I sit down to watch the event on television. Although the match itself does not start until three o'clock in the afternoon, the television presentation begins many hours before that. At about eleven o'clock in the morning the television networks swing into action. They begin with snapshots of the players and their families, show how each team got to the final, reveal what they had for breakfast, and other such trivia. This is followed by snippets of information about what types of shirts the players will wear, the state of the pitch and whether any players may be carrying slight injuries or not. Finally, after many hours viewing, the match itself begins. Because of the importance of the event and the nervousness of the players, the match itself is often of poor quality. Not alone that, but often the match goes to extra time in order to produce a result. This means that by the time the whole spectacle finishes I have been watching television for four or five hours. Without fail – on the evening of the event – I regularly feel dull, lifeless and washed out. Experience tells me this is likely to happen but time after time I fall into the same trap. One has to be both self-critical and honest if any change of behaviour has a chance of taking place.

Exactly the opposite happens to me on a regular basis. I make it a regular habit to go hiking up the mountains during the weekends and conditions before setting off can often seem most unappetising. Although I am tempted to call off the whole outing because the weather looks so poor, I know from experience that whatever effort I put in to ensure that the hike takes place will be more than rewarded. I have virtually never come home from a day's exertions on the hills without feeling exhilarated and delighted that I went even though the weather was less than clement.

When I contrast those two experiences I notice that the first, though eagerly anticipated, leaves me feeling unfulfilled, whereas the second – mountain walking and communing with nature, always abundantly repays the effort involved. It is only by giving oneself time, and reflecting on such experiences, that one may notice exactly what the spirit is trying to teach us. Often what you think is going to give you life doesn't in fact do so.

St Ignatius was a master of this type of discernment, and I believe Tony de Mello was also. They both suggested prayerful ways by which people could discover for themselves what was beneficial and what was harmful to them. They raised the following question: 'What element of prayer moved you?' By following that question you may discover more about your faith life and where God is trying to reach you. Another way of putting this is, 'Where in my life have I been finding fruit?' By returning to that spot and giving it the time and attention it deserves I may well derive profit for my inner spirit. St Ignatius himself was a past master and enlightening teacher when it came to matters of the soul. He explains in his autobiography how he himself was guided by the spirit so that he might discover and discern what ultimately would be good for him and for his soul and what was likely to do him permanent damage. He tells how, as a young man, he had no great interest in the life of the spirit. His life was centred around self-fulfilment. All this was brought to an abrupt halt however when he suffered a very serious leg injury whilst fighting for his local prince. As his very life was endangered, friends rushed him back to a sick bed in his own castle where he fought valiantly for his life over a six month period. He says himself that these six months were among the most important of his life. The spirit guided and taught him as a school teacher teaches his pupil. He learned to shift his allegiance from an earthly to a heavenly plane. He saw that God met him in everyday life situations. He found God in all things. So might we if we learn to observe ourselves and what truly gives us life.

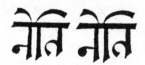

FINDING GOD IN YOUR FAVOURITE RIVERSIDE PLACE

Find a quiet time and place.

Quieten yourself, with your eyes closed.

Listen to the sounds around you.

Begin by concentrating on those sounds you can hear outside the room, such as wind, traffic, bird-song and the like.

Now draw your attention inwards to any sounds you can hear inside the room you are working in.

You may well hear the sound of other people and their breath patterns if there are others in the room or you may become conscious of any movements they make or you might hear the sound of music in the background. Try to ensure that these noises blur into the background and do not let them disturb you. After this draw the focus of your attention still farther inward and see if you can become aware of any noise going on inside yourself. You may be able to hear the sound of your own breath as it quietly comes through your nostrils or you may – if you have reached a great state of stillness by this point – manage to become aware of your heartbeat throbbing deep within you.

Keep your eyes closed and when you feel ready, start the fantasy exercise by going in your imagination to a favourite place of yours.

Use the following image: I imagine that I am walking on a long narrow roadway. It is a very busy roadway and I meet many people along the way who are rushing, fussing, talking loudly as they move along. All that can be heard are loud voices, and I am conscious of feeling uneasy with all this pushing and shoving.

I feel the need to escape and to break free.

I have a longing to be alone ... to be quiet within myself and to take some time away with Jesus.

After some minutes, the long narrow roadway takes on a more rural flavour and the people thin out. Their voices begin to die away and grow fainter. They merge and sink into the background. At this point I come to a clearing and notice before me a heavy silver gate which leads to my favourite place. There no people can be seen or heard. I can sense God's presence around me. As I walk through the gate I come into a countryside scene. There are fields around me with lambs playing in them. Cattle can also be heard grazing and even grasshoppers can be heard, though not seen, at their work. It is a warm bright day.

I feel the cool grass and the warm hard clay beneath my feet. I walk towards a glistening river which runs along the end of the field and through the clear water I can make out rocks and small reeds.

Eventually I come to my favourite spot where the river is forded by a man-made bridge and where one of the rocks – my favourite – juts up out of the water.

The rock is warm from the sun's rays so I make my way to it and sit down, feeling the soft and cold mud of the river-bed as my toes make contact. I throw a pebble into the still water and notice the ripples that spread out in a circle as a result of this action.

Eventually the ripples begin to fade and, as they do, they are replaced by a distorted face and figure in the water.

Unlike the ripples, this figure and face become ever clearer.

It is the face of Jesus.

I talk to Jesus and tell him everything that is troubling me.

This image of Jesus remains on the surface of the water while I talk to him.

After some time the face begins to fade and the water resumes its normal flow.

I thank Jesus for this time with him and begin my journey

back home – a more content and happy person than when I started out.

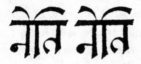

This establishes rhythm to your breathing and assists you prepare for a meditation session. Tony de Mello sometimes mentioned during his prayer workshops that one should not change one's breathing pattern but should hold to a regular rhythm taking about four seconds to breathe in and four seconds to breathe out. Try this pace for yourself and see if it is helpful.

First of all sit, stand or lie down with your back straight. Breathe though your nostrils and inhale slowly, steadily and deeply. As you work your way through each breath, inhale deeply and slowly, bringing the air right down to your lower abdomen so that you can feel your lower abdomen swell if you place your hand over your belly button. Then slowly allow your breath to exhale, up through the middle part of your lungs and complete the cycle of breath by allowing the air out through your upper chest and out through your mouth. The movement should be smooth and flowing. Do not force or tense yourself. Normally, the in breath takes about four seconds to complete, as does the out breath, with a very short pause between breathing in and breathing out.

Now relax.

As you breathe in, repeat the phrase 'Jesus, remember me' slowly and prayerfully. On the out breath, complete the sentence 'when you come into your kingdom' at the same pace. Repeat this exercise about eight times until you feel a rhythm building up and a relaxed feeling emerging. Just place yourself in Christ's presence. After a short time, you should be able to use this exercise easily enough. The first half of the exercise – the building up of a slow breath pattern – may be used as one form of introduction to many of the prayer exercises described in this book.

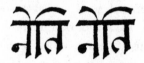

THE BLIND MAN
ST MARK'S GOSPEL (8: 22–26)

First slowly read the story of the blind man and his meeting with Jesus. Now take up a comfortable sitting position or lie flat on your back and make sure to wear loose clothing if possible. Become aware of your breathing and note how fast or slow it is and whether it is shallow or deep, smooth or jerky. Observe your breathing as if it were someone else who was taking in your breaths. As you breathe in, pick up the cool sensation of the air within your nostrils and follow it down your wind-pipe. Simply relax and try to be an impartial observer of your own breathing, as if it were not so much you who were breathing as you who were being breathed. Realise that God is giving you the priceless gift of life as you breathe in, so do not grab at it but accept it. Be still and allow God to go on giving you life. As you breathe out, relax completely and give God thanks for the life you receive.

Now I invite you to become the blind person. Try to think of how it would be for you if you were blind. Imagine getting up in the morning, trying to find your clothes, and think of the difficulties involved. Now imagine making yourself a cup of tea. How would you pour out the boiling water into your cup and how would you know when the water was coming close to the brim? What feelings arise within you as you accept the reality of your blindness? Do you feel sad, angry, depressed, lonely, or close to despair? Now try to move on from thoughts of your physical blindness to thoughts of your interior darkness. What is the darkness within you? Where are your blind spots? Are they spiritual, emotional, social or psychological? Now try to picture friends who have your best interests at heart. They let you know that Jesus is nearby. Who are these people? When they lead you to Jesus do you ask Him to take away your darkness or do they do the asking for you? Do you really believe Jesus can do something for you? Do you believe that He will? Remember that Jesus Himself told us, 'If you want something, ask for it'. When you are ready, give thanks for what you have received or may receive and slowly finish the exercise.

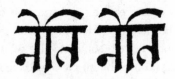

नेति नेति

Varada Mudra: 'The granting of blessings'
*One of the gestures frequently found in representations of the Buddha: it
symbolises his generosity in granting blessings.*

Prayer that brings life

So to pray as to deserve to be heard.

JANE AUSTEN

Tony de Mello came from a traditional Indian Catholic family. His Jesuit training relied first and foremost on the spirituality of St Ignatius of Loyola, the Order's founder. In time De Mello came to be recognised, especially among religious and priests, as a master in the use of the spiritual exercises of St Ignatius but in his workshops and retreats he sought the life of the spirit from a much wider variety of prayer styles. For that reason we will look now at different types of prayer in the hope that they may similarly motivate us. It's not an exhaustive list and even the types we do look at – contemplation, Ignatian meditation, fantasy exercises, Taize-style prayer, the Benedictine method of prayer, using a mantra or praying with icons, are often only touched upon. My objective is to give you some idea of the variety of prayer styles in the hope that you can choose for yourself the one that might be most helpful.

General comments

First, what is meditation? If you read books on prayer you will find many definitions but, for me, meditation is the process of relaxing my body and mind so that I can quietly go within myself to find my God or allow Him to find me. For this to happen I normally need to be in a quiet place, at least at first. Such places are not so easy to find today and we may be in danger of falling into one of two pitfalls. Either the noise which surrounds us may so dull us that we don't realise that we need periods of quiet in our lives, or, because of the wall-to-wall noise which often envelops us, we may be incapable of handling silent spaces even when they are quite adjacent.

The meditation sphere is a space that helps us focus on what is important in our lives. It helps us to find a pathway to the centre of ourselves. Thomas Merton, the Trappist monk, said meditation has no point and no reality unless it is firmly rooted in life. So one of the purposes of meditation is to nourish and enrich our everyday living, our relationships with others, with God and with life in general.

The need for such a space in our lives grows more acute as the pace of life hots up. Many business people and artists, not to mention sports personalities and pop stars have highlighted the danger of allowing your life run you, instead of you running your life. In the 1960s, the English pop superstars, the Beatles, found themselves a maharishi at the Academy of Meditation in the Himalayan foothills, who told them, 'I teach a simple system of meditation, which gives people an insight into life and allows them to enjoy both peace and happiness'.

This is exactly what the Beatles felt they needed at that time if they were to retain any semblance of control over their lives. They described the teachings of their guru thus: 'We meditated for about five hours a day in all, two hours in the morning and perhaps three hours in the evening and the rest of the time we slept, ate, sun-bathed and had fun. You just sit down, relax and then you repeat a sound to yourself and that is all it is, there is nothing more to it'.

A few years ago I made a retreat myself in an ashram in India where those with heavy work-loads came to refresh themselves. The advice given there was remarkably similar to the above. You were advised to slow down, so that you might come to your senses and balance the different elements in your life. It was explained to us that the eastern search for God is directed within the individual whereas the western search is directed outside. The western tradition holds that God is separate from man, superior to him, but this is not the case in the east. In particular in China they stress more the balancing of Yang and Yin – the masculine and feminine – but how are we to achieve this balance?

We can make a start with prayer. Those of you who are familiar with the enneagram will know that human beings are said to operate out of one of three centres. Some of us operate out of the head, others the heart, while still others find that their drive comes from the gut. To explain what I mean by the 'head', 'heart' and 'gut' human centres, a short illustration may be helpful.

A story is told of a school bus trip that takes place during the summer break. Unfortunately, during the journey, the bus crashes and steam and smoke begin to pour from the engine. The 'head' people are said to respond to the situation by standing up in the bus, counting the children to make sure they are all right, before dividing them into separate groups, and sending them under the direction of the teachers out the front and back doors. Very efficient, very heady. The 'heart' people, by contrast, gather the children to themselves, hug them, comfort them and soothe their fears. Very caring, but the bus may well have gone up in flames by the time any definite action is taken. The 'gut' people's action is just to jump off the bus themselves.

Enneagram experts sometimes suggest that 'head', 'heart' and 'gut' people are most helped by the three types of prayer I am going to outline below. However, I have found from participants of prayer weekends that a more helpful suggestion may be that we all go through different phases in our lives and that the varying prayer styles outlined may help us as those different moods take effect.

PRAYER TYPE ONE — NOVICESHIP-STYLE PRAYER

This first type of prayer might more accurately be called the Ignatian meditation method but I call it the noviceship style because it was the type which was shown to us and almost exclusively used in our Jesuit noviceship. Shortly after we arrived to begin our training as Jesuits, we were allocated an 'Angelus' or guardian angel. This guide was someone who would counsel us in the ways of prayer. An expert, you might say. In truth, our expert was a second-year fellow novice who had an extra year's prayer experience under his belt. The guardian angel's task was to train us in the ways of meditation and this consisted of the following. Firstly, our guide chose for us a gospel passage. This was often the gospel taken from the mass of the following day, and in an allocated period of about half an hour, he read the passage for us and drew out from it a number of points which he thought might be worth reflecting on. This prayerful reflection was to be done the following morning. Let me give an example. Perhaps my spiritual guide might have chosen the beautiful passage about the disciples on the road to Emmaus from St Luke's gospel. Having read the script, he would begin to divide the text into five sections, gleaning a message from each section, in something like the following manner.

Point One. Two people were making their way along the road to Emmaus with their faces downcast. My guide would suggest that when I attempt a meditation on this text the following morning, I might reflect back over the past year of my life and think of times when I also was on life's path trying to make my way to God, but feeling low or forsaken with my own face downcast.

Point Two. Suddenly, without noticing Him, Jesus appears into their lives. Here, my guide would ask me to consider whether perhaps Jesus had also made his presence felt in my life, and was I as unobservant about that fact as the disciples had been along the road?

Point Three. As the two disciples walked along, Christ began to explain many things to them, so that, without really being aware, their humour and spirits rose and, by the time it came towards evening, they were begging the stranger to stay with them. My spiritual guide would suggest that perhaps Christ had worked the same miracle for us. Maybe we also had been enthused or energised without really noticing the process taking place.

Point Four. After the disciples had persuaded Jesus to come in and have a meal with them they caught a glimpse of His presence in the breaking of the bread, but almost as soon as they recognised His presence, He was already gone from their midst. My guide would suggest that we also may have had intimations of Christ's presence within our lives – nothing definite, you understand, but delicate hints because Christ works in subtle ways.

Point Five. When they realised that Christ had been with them, the disciples got up and ran back along the road they had come in order to share the news with their companions. My guide might ask me to think and pray about what I had done with the gift of faith I had been given.

That roughly describes what I call the Noviceship or Ignatian meditation process. In this format, one follows closely the gospel story, drawing out the relevant points for consideration and applying those points to one's own life. It is very Ignatian in structure in that it follows closely one of the methods described by St Ignatius of Loyola in his spiritual exercises and many find it a helpful method when prayer times are tough.

PRAYER TYPE TWO – CONTEMPLATION

A more intimate form of prayer than the above, but one that also involves a heavy reliance on scripture, is called contemplation, Ignatian contemplation or gospel contemplation. It makes use of guided imagery and active imagination within the framework of a gospel passage of Jesus' life. Using this method, one again chooses a scene from the gospels but instead of viewing it from the outside as one might a film or video, in this instance, one steps inside the frame and becomes part of the action oneself. You picture yourself on the road to Emmaus with the disciples. You listen to their conversation, sense or feel their disappointment with life, and become vaguely aware when Jesus enters the frame. You feel your own spirits lift and hear Jesus asking you why you are so down-hearted. You begin a conversation with Christ and try to dialogue with Him. You use all your senses insofar as you are able to and gain what spiritual profit you can from the intimate encounter.

PRAYER TYPE THREE – TAIZE-STYLE PRAYER
I call the third style of prayer the Taize method because it is the type of prayer which is used almost exclusively in the Ecumenical Youth prayer centre at Taize, France. In essence it involves the continuous use of a line from scripture, sung slowly, and repeated over and over again. The prayerful effects of this chanting are greatly assisted by aids which you provide to colour or enhance the ambience. Thus the room is carefully chosen, candles are normally lit, the lighting is very subdued and incense may well be used to heighten the atmosphere. The effects of the continuous scriptural passage or line chanted over and over again tend to bring the participant into a quieter or more sacred space where our paths and that of Christ may meet. This method closely resembles the Benedictine method described by Tony de Mello in his book *Sadhana*, and it is not too dissimilar to a method used by the ancient Irish monks in their monasteries. As Fr John Veltri, a Canadian Jesuit, describes it, the monks, upon waking, filed down the corridors to a central meeting room. There they sat quietly until one of them, standing at a lectern, began to read a passage from the gospels. He read clearly in a leisurely manner for a short time and then

paused for thirty or forty seconds. Then he re-read the same passage in the same clear, leisurely style. Again, he paused for half a minute or so and then read the same passage for a third time. When he paused this time, some of the monks began to return to their cells in order to pray over the passage. Others waited for the fourth reading and even the fifth before they, too, left for their cells. What was happening? These repetitive readings saturated the monks imaginations by means of a gospel scene or phrase of particular energy and colour. This saturation would, of course, minimise distractions, and encourage a frame of mind and heart conducive to prayer.

PRAYER TYPE FOUR – 'JUST BE' PRAYER.
I call this fourth type of prayer the 'just be' style because of an incident that happened to me some years ago. I was beginning to get a bit tired of the Ignatian meditation method of prayer and decided to ask a wise and saintly Franciscan if he would direct me on my annual retreat. Having told me that he knew nothing about prayer-direction, he finally agreed to undertake the task and suggested we start the retreat straight away with a walk along the Donegal coast. During this walk he suggested that I should explain to him how I normally prayed and where God had been active in my life during the past year. I therefore began our conversation with a long rigmarole about how I prayed, and explained in some detail the intricacies of the Ignatian meditation method. He looked bemused and was not at all impressed.

'But when do you get down to the prayer?' he kept asking.

Finally, in desperation, I asked him what he did during his own prayer.

'Ah, I just be,' he explained, 'and if I am a bit distracted I might take a couple of words from the scriptures and then "just be" again with the Lord.'

This 'just be' style of prayer is almost as difficult to describe as it is to undertake. I've heard numbers of experienced people attempt to describe it in the following terms: 'I sit in front of the Tabernacle, and I just look at Him while He just looks at me'.

Other methods of prayer which may be helpful:

THE MANTRA

This is not unlike the Benedictine method of prayer which uses a phase from the scriptures to help focus one's thought. In the eastern cultures people are often given a sound to help them pray. Buddhist chant, Taize chant and Gregorian chant all underline the importance of sound. They all use this medium to help the participant into interior silence. The sound given is usually a phrase that's chanted, sung, hummed or even just heard as a sound within the mind to stimulate the calmness which is desired within meditation. Normally the sound given is a phrase invoking the name of God and it might be described as a technique for focusing attention, allowing all other thoughts, distractions, concerns or worries to stand aside. A single word or phrase repeated over and over as a focus for thoughts, the Mantra exists in both eastern and western cultures. For example, in the east, the word, *Aum,* is often used. Each letter of the word A-U-M is assigned to one of the major Hindu gods. The letter A is assigned to Brahma, the creator. U is given to Vishnu, the preserver. The letter M is assigned to Shiva, the destroyer. Thus, in the east the *Aum* Mantra represents the whole cycle of creation and it is found both in Buddhism and Hinduism. The sound is repeated slowly and deeply – it is vibrated – so that it resonates. Some say the Mantra should be a sound totally without meaning, others that it should stand for peace or God. Fr Lawrence Freeman, a Benedictine priest and expert on the Mantra style of prayer, says that the only important thing is that the words chosen should be wholly right for the user.

In 1954 John Main, the well-known Catholic spiritual writer, was taught by a holy Indian teacher in Malaya to repeat a single Christian phrase for the time of his meditation, two separate half hours each day. He was told to sit down, be still, close his eyes lightly, be relaxed but alert. Then he should silently, interiorly, begin to say a single word. He was recommended to use the Aramaic phrase, *Maranatha* which means 'Lord, come' and he advised his followers to do the same. Sometimes he synchronised this word with his breath pattern. He said: Listen to the word as you say it, gently but continuously. Do not think or imagine anything, spiritual or otherwise. If thoughts and images come, these are distractions at the time of meditation, so keep returning to the simple work of saying the word. Whatever thoughts, ideas or images float across your mind, let them float away. Whatever great insights come to you, let them go too. Save them for another time. Whatever the distractions, simply return to saying your word. Repetition purifies. Probably, to begin with, you are likely to encounter restlessness and discontentment. We are so geared to plan for the future, or regret mistakes of the past that we miss the present. Missing that we miss everything

In the Indian ashrams some people go to the guru or holy leader to receive their own personal Mantra whilst others try out different phrases until they find one that feels right. Fr John Main, who was one of those who popularised the Mantra style of prayer in the west, believed deeply that we learn best from our own life experiences and that at times in everyone's life there are moments of crisis, loss, death, separation, or disaster which must be faced and meditated through. He stressed the importance of being faithful to prayer and meditation in our ordinary time so that we can be prepared for times of crisis. 'Being faithful to your time of prayer,' he said, 'is a little like paying your insurance premiums in good times and bad for if you don't pay your premiums in the good days then when, and if, the going gets tough there is nothing in reserve to cover your difficulties'. So in Mantra style prayer be alert, upright, but at all times be relaxed and it may help to close your eyes. Let the face, shoulders, neck and body relax for you should be at ease. Then silently, interiorly, in your mind and heart, simply begin to repeat your word or Mantra. When you say the word listen to it and give it your full attention. It is by saying the word that you obtain silence. If any thoughts come into your mind let them go. This is not a time for thinking. Just let go and keep returning humbly and faithfully to the Mantra word you have been given or chosen. The silence changes, or could change, your image of Jesus and may give you a deeper relationship with Him. Do not be discouraged if praying seems difficult. God will speak to you in his own way.

It is important after stillness to have a formalised way of returning to the hustle and bustle of normal life so avoiding the sudden shock of coming back to the here and now too abruptly, as this can cause physical discomfort, dizziness, or confusion. The return to daily living after a period of quiet prayer should be done gently and gradually. I have noticed, particularly with schoolchildren, that if sufficient time and attention is not given to the winding down phase, the result may be a feeling of dullness and sleepiness immediately after the meditation session.

WHAT ARE THE DIFFICULTIES in these types of prayer and meditation? Whilst most spiritual writers encourage us by saying that the practice of prayer puts us in touch with our deepest, innermost selves and with our God, few would deny that much time is spent being disappointed over our progress. Many of us are daunted by the hard work involved and there may be very little apparent change within us. Perhaps people look for results too quickly. It may be that change only comes over a period of time and even then not in a way, or at a pace, that we anticipated. Cardinal Basil Hume, the English Benedictine, has said that God does not always speak to us in times of prayer but what He does do is soften the ground, so to speak, during prayer time so that fertile growth can take place outside the time of prayer.

We may also be disheartened by distractions which seem to occur with disturbing frequency during prayer time. We cannot stop our minds wandering and we feel like someone taking a puppy-dog for a walk. Just as the puppy-dog seems to be leading the owner on a merry dance, so it seems that our distractions are in control of us, rather than our being in control of them. I remember a Zen priest saying whenever distracting thoughts invaded his thought he made no attempt to cast them away. He simply left them to depart of their own accord. He used an old Indian proverb to give his listeners courage: 'You cannot prevent birds flying around your head, but you can stop them nesting in your hair'.

But if the difficulties of prayer are readily apparent, so too are the benefits. We may be helped both to suppress the clamour which often seems to reside in our heads and to create a calm space in our hearts, as well as open up a space within ourselves where we can talk with our God, and with our deepest selves.

The invitation to deepen our hearts and our silence is an invitation to everybody – not just to those of a contemplative nature. If we can instil in ourselves the courage of quiet, of listening, and the belief that we are spoken to in our hearts by the Lord, then other difficulties may subside or be lessened. As Christ Himself said, 'if only you knew who it was that was speaking to you, you too would ask for the living water for it leads to eternal life'.

THE JESUS PRAYER

This prayer form apparently dates from the earliest centuries of the Church's history but it was little known or practised until the publication in the west of *The Way of a Pilgrim* around 1925. The nineteenth century Russian pilgrim who wrote this book speaks of his discovery of the secret of uninterrupted prayer. Tony de Mello is credited by Fr Valles, a Spanish Jesuit working in India, with introducing Indian Christians to the use of the Jesus Prayer. The method employed is to take the phrase 'Lord Jesus Christ, Son of God, have mercy on me, a sinner' and to use it as a sort of Mantra. These words are repeated continuously by the mind in the heart and thus the prayer format is also sometimes known by the term 'prayer of the heart'.

USING AN ICON

In this type of prayer you simply place the image before you, whether it be a crucifix, icon, Taize cross or other religious object and when your mind begins to wander you draw it back to the subject under review by returning your gaze to the icon.

FANTASY PRAYER EXERCISES

This is a technique which gives back the imagination to the individual. It is a style of prayer greatly favoured by Fr Tony de Mello for it facilitates us in looking at parts of ourselves which otherwise might be too threatening. It also helps us to find God in situations where otherwise He might pass unnoticed. If you work with youth groups you may notice that some young people, as well as some adults, have a fantasy life that is far more vivid than that experienced by the rest of us. For the majority of people, mental images are pale and fleeting things and some experience difficulty with this type of prayer. However it appears that a few people are able to conjure up experiences, complete with smells, sound and body sensations that are almost hallucinatory in their detail. With a little practice, most people can derive a good deal of profit and enjoyment from this type of prayer. At the end of each chapter, I give an example of a fantasy exercise which should not be too demanding for the reader.

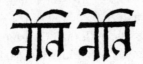

Simple Meditation for Breathing

Meditation is a natural experience which opens you to your own source of energy and insight. It involves the art of 'just being' and thus provides a sort of counter-balance to the constant pressure of forever 'doing'. Many of us lead lives full of pressure – driving us to work, to talk, to succeed, to fulfil responsibilities, to avoid failure, to consume ever more and more. A short period of meditation can help to lessen the destructive effects of these pressures.

Try this short meditation on breath
Become aware of your breathing and begin to breath, slowly and deeply, with lips closed, both inhaling and exhaling through the nose ... count the breaths, thinking of nothing save the counting ... begin counting the breaths ... up to ten ... then begin again at one, going up to ten again ... keep your mind on the breath count ... in this way you may quieten a racing mind.

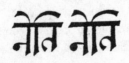

BODY AWARENESS MEDITATION

Relax into a comfortable position ...

Pay attention to how your body is ... to your position ... your feelings ... your sensations ...

Start from the tip of your head ... to your face ... your shoulders ... your trunk ... legs ... feet ... point of contact with the chair or floor ... really feel it ... take your time ...

Now make a slower journey through your body ... feet ... legs ... buttocks ... belly ... back ... chest ... hands ... arms ... neck ... face ... head ...

Simply feel the sensations which exist in each part of your body ... take lots of time with this exercise ... Let things be ... just feel ... and let go.

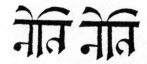

MEDITATION ON A CANDLE

Light a candle and begin to picture it in your imagination.

Note its size, how it warms and lightens the room ...

The flame flickers and is blown off course by the gentle breeze but it constantly returns to its upright stance.

It is not blown completely off course despite the fact that it is neither powerful nor important.

However dark it may be, the candle is never overcome by the darkness.

The wick appears to be on fire, but it is not itself destroyed by fire.

Now I begin to imagine that I am a candle.

How many of the candle's attributes apply to me?

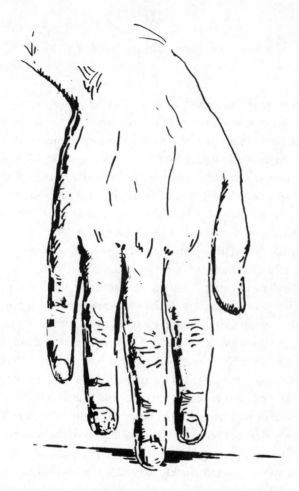

The Earth-Touching Posture:

While sitting immovably in meditation the voice of Dharma challenged the Buddha with neglect of his social duties. In response, as if calling the Earth to witness his right to be there, Buddha gestured with his right hand, letting the fingertips touch the earth.

FINDING FOCUS IN YOUR LIFE

Within the silence one touches the Heart of God.

WHITE EAGLE

Every year, in my family, when I was young, our parents took us on a fortnight's holiday and the occasion was always a great event. Like other families, I suppose, a time comes when children want to go off and holiday on their own and I well remember the year this happened for me. My younger brother and I were aged thirteen and fourteen at the time and we felt that a hitch-hiking trip around Ireland would be both exciting and adventurous for us. Thus we presented a detailed itinerary to my father and after some deliberation and consultation with my mother, he finally gave his permission.

Day one of our holiday saw us starting out by local bus to the village of Enniskerry at the very outskirts of Dublin. Although we intended hitch-hiking, we thought we should at least give ourselves a bit of a start by bus. That was about as far as our knowledge of hitch-hiking or travel went. We took up our hitching station right in the middle of the village where the bus stopped, and proceeded to stick out our thumbs. For the first hour or so, this procedure seemed quite exciting and it only slowly dawned on us that no vehicle seemed the remotest bit interested in stopping for us. As we grew colder and more despondent, our interest quickly flagged. At the end of our second hour's efforts, with still no sign of a lift in sight, the heavens began to open and heavy rain set in. That finished us. Whether my younger brother's nerve or mine failed first I cannot now recall, but a joint decision was arrived at that perhaps this type of hitch-hiking holiday was not such a bright idea after all. Maybe we should abandon our plans and row in with the family holiday. We walked back to the local phone-box to ring my mother and let her know of the change of plans, and as I was the older brother I was commissioned to make the call.

Now normally on Saturday afternoon – and this was a Saturday – my mother would be cooking in the kitchen and my father would be safely out of doors working in the garden so I was taken completely by surprise when my phone-call was answered by my father who must have come indoors because of the rain. I began hurriedly to explain how we were now hitching on the road. Despite our best efforts cars did not appear to be stopping and I explained that my brother and I had decided in our best wisdom to abandon our plans and come home instead. 'If you started out, keep going', was the only reply my father made, and I then heard the bang of the phone being put down at the other end. As soon as I got out of the phone-box my brother asked me what our mother had said. 'She didn't say anything because it was our father who answered, and he just said, "if you started out, keep going".'

The message was a hard one, but one that has come back to me many times in later life. When you feel like giving up, don't quit. Whenever I tell that story now, people ask was the holiday not a disaster? Certainly not. When we forced ourselves back on to the road – we really had little enough option – a car stopped almost immediately and the driver quickly saw that we were both young and inexperienced. He told us first that, when hitch-hiking, we needed to get out a bit from the village or town to a spot where we could easily be noticed by drivers and where they could stop safely. When he heard what an out-of-the-way youth hostel we were aiming for, he took further pity on us and drove us straight to the location. After a good night's sleep and a hearty breakfast we scarcely looked back and toured the country like seasoned professionals arriving back home a couple of weeks later very full of ourselves. My mother was delighted with the account of our successful travels and when my father came home some little time later she recounted our triumphs. The first day's telephone-call was never mentioned by him and I discovered years later from my mother that he never told her anything about it at the time. So, a useful motto for our prayer life might be, 'If you started out, keep going', and that's not an easy thing to do. Almost all those who attempt to pray are faced with moments of doubt, disillusionment, darkness, distraction and maybe even despair. Many times you will feel like giving up. Christ Himself must have been acutely aware of that danger when he chose Peter to lead his followers. He knew how often the going would get tough. He knew how often His band of disciples would be tempted towards desertion. But He also knew Peter's resolve. He had seen Peter's granite-like qualities and placed his trust in these. We might ask for some of Peter's determination in our own prayer.

In the previous chapter we looked over some forms of prayer that might be helpful. Both St Ignatius of Loyola and Fr Tony de Mello highlighted one form of prayer that might assist us when we feel like giving up. Tony de Mello normally called it fantasy prayer; others have termed it 'Ignatian Imaginary'. This prayer of the imagination can either be gospel-based or not but in either case the participants – by entering into the fantasy – may discover something deep within themselves.

Henri Matisse, the artist, was visited on one occasion by a friend whose nerves were frayed and frazzled. Matisse said to him, 'Andre, you must find the artichokes in your life'. With that saying he brought his friend down to the artichoke patch in his garden and told him that each day after he had worked hard he felt the need to get his life back into focus. 'I need to be still and meditate. I need a ritual that inspires me, relaxes me, gives me a new perspective towards my work. Everybody needs to find the artichoke-patch'.

Recently I was giving some workshops in Africa and was told about some of the exploratory trips the adventurer, Cecil Rhodes, made to uncover hidden areas of Africa. It was said of him that he pushed both his comrades and baggage-handlers to their very limit. On one such trip, after a couple of days of endless marching, the natives, who had been rushed through the jungle with white man's speed, suddenly dropped their loads to the ground saying, 'We will not go a step further at present for we have come so far and so fast that we must now allow our spirits to catch up with our bodies'.

Both what the African natives sought, and what Henri Matisse found in his patch of artichokes, is what millions of people are searching for as we approach the year two thousand. They seek serenity and a sense of God in an age of stress. This is particularly true of today's young people but it may not be readily apparent to them. It seems that they can only be led to a realisation of this need very slowly and one way of leading them to this awareness is through fantasy exercises.

But what are these fantasy exercises and how can we introduce them to ourselves and others? When are they most useful? At various times in our lives, moments of pain, bereavement, particular stress, or even just plain listlessness, fantasy-style prayer may come to your rescue where nothing else seems worthwhile. Tell your mind to take a mental holiday. Take time out to create a short break – time to be serene, refreshed and re-energised. Many of the older teenagers I work with find this particularly helpful during their tiring school week. In your mind you create a quiet and safe place where you can be alone with your deepest self and with your God. You may revisit this space or place as often as you like once you have created it.

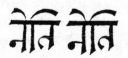

In order to see how this might work, in reality, take a little time out to try the following exercise.

Find a suitable place by yourself, sit down and close you eyes. Breath quietly and slowly and allow your whole body to relax. If it's possible, use quiet music to hold your fantasy in place. When you have become quietened, visualise something that is relaxing and enjoyable. You might picture yourself in your favourite place, or beside a river or beach of your choice. Use your imagination to colour in the weather. It may be a golden summer's day or you may find yourself in the quiet shadows of evening. In any case, choose for your fantasy somewhere you feel safe. When you have got such a vision in your mind's eye – explore.

Deepen your awareness of your senses. Can you smell anything? What sounds can you hear? Note the time of day, whether it is morning or evening or mid-day: can you feel the heat of the sun ray's on your body?

Be aware of yourself in the fantasy. Where are you? Are you sitting up or lying down? Take time with each step and allow the scene to develop in your imagination. Feel at peace and refreshed by the fantasy and when you are finished, slowly come back to the present place and open your eyes.

I KNOW THAT FOR some people the whole notion of using fantasy meditation as a means of prayer is puzzling. For others, their problem is that they find it difficult to get their imagination working at all. Fr Mark Link, of the United States, one of the best-known Jesuit writers on modern spirituality, says that he attempted a programme of fantasy meditations with some doubting teenagers quite recently and the impact of his year-long course was truly remarkable. Working with senior pupils in an Irish school, I have been similarly surprised with the ease with which they take to the sessions. I should mention here that any mention of gospel or Jesus at an early stage of the undertaking brings a chorus of disapproval and a rapid end to the proceedings but perhaps mine are a particularly heathen lot!

So how should you start out with a fantasy exercise either on your own or with a group? I usually start by introducing the notion of relaxation to the group and stressing how important finding time and space can be if we wish God to speak in our lives. I might mention the scene from the Book of Samuel (Chapter three), where the boy Samuel and his master need to be alive to the possibility of God's word in their lives; or I might describe how Christ Himself needed periods of quiet and reflection in His life, as shown by His sojourn in the desert.

In order that individuals or group members might have a gentle introduction to a fantasy exercise, I ask participants to close their eyes, quieten their minds and hearts by means of one of the breathing exercises described earlier and then, as if they were rewinding a video, they should play back the last week of their lives as if on a screen in their imaginations. Most people can do this readily enough. You only have to go back over the events which occurred in your life during the past week: remember whom you met, what your moods were in the various situations you encountered, and where you noticed Christ or were noticed by Him in all of this – if at all. Reviewing one's life was a theme regularly mentioned and favoured by St Ignatius of Loyola. Fr Tony de Mello also recommended exercises of this sort in his Sadhana Prayer Centre. He told people to go over their lives and find out where they had found spiritual fruit in the recent past, for the outer changes in their lives might be clear but the inner changes might be less obvious.

To find out about these inner changes, it helps to take the step into silence, for this is at the threshold of all real prayer: 'Be still and know that I am God'. As Jesus Himself said, 'do not use many words when you pray but enter into your room and be still'. The invitation to deepen our hearts and our silence is an invitation to everybody, not just those of a contemplative nature, for it is the same offer as was made to the woman at the well, 'if only you knew who it was that was speaking to you, you too would ask for the living water'.

So I suggest to the groups I am working with that they let silence quieten their spirits. In this way I hope that the Lord may come to take His place in the void that has been created. More and more these days I believe people are expressing a hunger within themselves and a longing for a central point of stillness within their lives. It is as if their lives were like a warped cartwheel. As with the cartwheel if it is not properly balanced or the spokes are of unequal strength – the whole operation is out of kilter. Many seem to feel a little like Scrooge in Dickens' *A Christmas Carol.* Just as Scrooge keeps himself busy in order not to notice what is truly going on within his life, so many of us also move at great speed in our search for happiness. The speed and the bustle are the very things that hide what's important.

What may happen when you quieten yourself during a fantasy exercise? Well, just as muddy water, if it is left to settle becomes still and clarifies itself, so we too, if we give ourselves space and silence, may begin to see what's really important in our lives. A brief story may illustrate this.

Recently, a young woman asked her spiritual director if she could take on prayer in her life on a daily basis for a year's duration as she had some decisions in her life that she really needed to pray through. She explained that she had spent quite some time in India working as a lay missionary but that during that time she had fallen in love twice and become engaged to the two men involved. In both cases she really felt the two men were ideal life partners for her but as the relationships became more and more serious, both men had broken the engagement and run away. Now she wished to decide whether she should return to India and devote her life to being a lay missionary or whether she should remain open one more time to the idea of a permanent relationship. Both paths held some attraction for her. Thus she started on her daily diet of prayer, always keeping the same question at the back of her mind. 'What is it about me that made the two men run away?' For months she prayed over the issue, looking for an answer. Each week she talked over what was happening during the prayer with her spiritual director and as no answer came he continually sent her back to renew her quest. At last, after about six months, came the breakthrough. When the director asked her why the two men had run away from relationships with her, she replied: 'That was always my question, but it was the wrong one. They never ran away. I ran away'. In the stillness and quiet of the fantasy exercises she was undertaking, she was able to come to a deeper realisation about herself and discover that being a freedom-loving and risk-taking individual, as well as one who lived life to the full, she was fearful that the married state might restrict her style and bring her unhappiness. Thus, unconsciously, she had run away from the two relationships and the men, sensing this fact almost as soon as it happened and before the young woman herself knew it, terminated the relationship before they themselves got emotionally hurt.

FANTASY MEDITATIONS ARE SOMETIMES difficult to undertake but they do have the power to open up areas of our lives that would otherwise remain hidden and which we might well find too painful to face head on. Participants at prayer weekends express this in different ways. At a recent workshop one person was forthright enough to admit: 'When the fantasy meditation started I was very confused first of all, then I got tired ... then I went my own way'. That's a very honest report and a beautiful example of how God and ourselves sometimes interact in prayer. Another said, 'I fell asleep just when it got to the most dangerous bit for me. If I had not pointed this out myself and the director of prayer had mentioned it first, I think I would have got annoyed'. A third said, 'Essentially I feel fantasy meditations are a trip into my deepest self where either with Jesus or just on my own, I discover more about who I am and what the purpose of my life is'.

One man who spent some time in the east and studied with a Buddhist master gave some cautionary hints to his fellow prayer travellers. 'I was told I always wanted to know the answers, like someone who wants to know the temperature of water, the density of it and why it's transparent. "One day I will just push you in", the master told me, "for this monkey mind of yours must be stilled before anything worthwhile happens".'

When your mind has become still some questions may begin to float to the surface. You may begin to ask yourself about facets of the past year of your life: What challenged me? What did I learn from my community or from living with my family? What areas of my life needed to grow?

With reflection, did I see any blind spots or areas in my life that needed extra time or attention? What were my gifts to the community? What gave me life? What deadened me over the last month or year? What were the low points during the past year? What were the high points? What have I not resolved? What do I wish I had done differently? What am I glad I did? Where was Christ in my life?

None of these questions are easy to answer. Trying to find out what you truly want in life or what God may want of you is no simple matter. It requires effort. St Francis Xavier noted this in one of his many letters. 'You will find God if you do not neglect your daily knowledge of yourself'. Twice a day Xavier engaged in a sort of fantasy exercise by looking with the eyes of his heart at the concrete day he had just been through. There he tried to discover where exactly God had been present in his affairs. He took his day and examined it from three viewpoints: thanks, sorrow and hope. He suggested one should decide first what one wanted to thank the Lord for that day, then go over the day's events expressing sorrow for the times when one had let oneself and the Lord down, and finally go on to hope that one might be more actively present to the Lord in the day ahead. St Francis Xavier changed his life with this simple practice for he understood that you don't become a saint by what you do alone but by the quality with which you do it. The Cistercian monk, Thomas Merton, advised something similar and added, 'Ask me not where I live or what I eat but what I am living for, and ask me what I think is keeping me from living fully'.

So, silence and fantasy-style meditation may assist us in lessening the noise and confusion of our days and make them not only bearable but also help us to focus, relax, slow down, get a handle on our lives, and even help to make sense of whatever mess may be occurring. We are not alone in the struggle. God has plans and may want to make a few changes too. Use of fantasies and imagination allied to a certain amount of prayerful reflection about the past can enrich our lives, make God's plan for us more lucid and encourage us towards the future.

THE TEMPLE MEDITATION ...

This is an interesting fantasy exercise. When I first worked on it with a group during a workshop, a woman who lived with her husband in her mother-in-law's house for many years told me a story about a previous workshop she had attended. She was asked to imagine a temple. During her prayer, a dream-like sequence inserted itself in her mind during which an extra wing suddenly appeared alongside the building she pictured. This space appeared to her to have great potential. However she felt restricted in her movements from ever getting into it. Some months after the workshop and very shortly after her mother-in-law died, she wrote to tell me that the dream had recurred during her prayer time and she realised she now owned her own house as her mother-in-law had departed. She no longer needed to dream of extra potential any more.

Now try the exercise for yourself.

Prepare yourself by means of a listening exercise. Settle down by finding a position in which you are alert and relaxed. Take a few deep breaths and then listen carefully to sounds outside the room. Just note these sounds. They may be traffic or bird-song or wind. Slowly allow these sounds fade into the background as you now begin to focus your attention on sounds inside the room. You may pick up the sound of background music, or the voice of the group leader, or another's movement. Now try to bring the focus of your attention still farther inward and listen for any sounds you can hear inside yourself. At first you may hear nothing. Then slowly you may begin to make out the sound of air coming into your body through your nostrils. You may even become aware of your own heartbeat. Let the sounds and the silence relax you. Then let your imagination get to work. Imagine you are walking along a country lane and in the distance you see a temple. You make your way towards it and as

your curiosity is aroused you make your way up the long winding entrance steps. These steps lead to a entrance hall with many
doors leading off it and you choose one of the doors and make
your way through. You find yourself in a yellow room and as
you stand there the room becomes full of yellow light. Breathe
in this yellow light. As you are breathing in a friend comes in
and takes you by the hand and leads you to a room filled with
books. Each book has a name on it and your friend brings you
down the rows until you reach a book that has your name on
the cover. What is the book like? After some time your friend
tells you that there is a message on the fly-leaf of the book and
the message is especially for you. You read it. You may talk to
your friend about any worries or problems you have. You can
tell him/her anything you like. When you are ready to leave,
your friend gives you the message in your hands and you go
back to the yellow room. Yellow represents peace for you. Now
take leave of your friend and go back to the entrance hall, down
the steps of the temple and back along the country lane. When
you find yourself near the end of the lane open your eyes and
have a good stretch, allowing your eyes become accustomed to
the light.

Important note. As the meditation leader, your preparation
is important to the success of a guided meditation. Pray the
meditation before leading the group through it. In this way you
will become comfortable with its style and content. Praying the
meditation beforehand can also help you to set the right mood
for yourself and the group and it leaves you feeling confident
that you will give any necessary directions in good time. If you
intend to guide the meditation yourself, allow sufficient time
for the imagery to take hold and for prayerful reflection afterwards.

THE MIRROR MEDITATION

Quieten yourself by means of one of the preparatory exercises.

Now imagine that you are walking through a field. It is springtime and you see ahead of you a narrow path that leads to the top of a rising hill. As you reach the top you come upon a long mirror, standing upright and you notice that the mirror faces the full sun. You walk around the mirror and notice that it has lost pieces of its silvering. It is chipped in one place. You are surprised to find the mirror in this place and wonder what it might mean. Now walk around to the front of the mirror. Its face is liquid with light. It throws off so much light that you would go blind if you were to look at it directly. The sun pours its light on to the mirror, holding nothing back of its power and brilliance. The mirror accepts the sun's light, taking as much as it possibly can. It does not let its little and large flaws matter. They are insignificant compared to the light which the mirror accepts. Then the mirror throws back to the sun all the light that melts in its heart. It holds no light back. Now turn your face to the sun. You are now receiving the sun's light, taking all you can and you ignore any flaws that might hinder your sense of receiving.

Now slowly realise how similar all this is to the interaction between God and yourself. God is the sun. You are the mirror. God pours into you many gifts and you become a partaker in God's actions in the world insofar as you can. You rest in this exchange of sunlight and love.

Invite yourself to relax and settle into one of the recommended prayer positions. Take slow and deep breaths and then let them go with a full sigh. Continue with these slow and deep breaths for a couple of minutes. Imagine these breaths as they come through your nostrils and right down to your belly button. Relax as you breath out and let the breath flow easily. Your awareness is now focused on your natural breathing. Allow each breath to enter and depart deeply at its own pace. Concentrate at the beginning on following the flow of your breath as it comes in through your nostrils, then settles, and slowly is exhaled through your mouth.

Place yourself in the presence of God and allow yourself become quiet. Now use your imagination to picture yourself alone on a sea shore. There may be many things in your life that have grown far too big of late, so search out what these elements might be. Equally, there may be important aspects of your life that you are ignoring.

Ask the Lord now for quiet and peace in your life. How will these come? Seek solitude, for this gift may allow time for important decisions to be made. Are there decisions you are running away from?

Move on from the sea shore. In your imagination place yourself in your own grave and look at how decisions you are making in your life at present may appear from there.

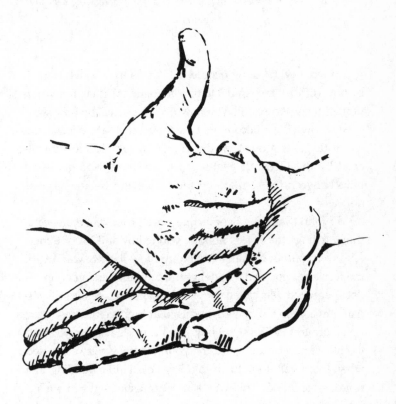

This Mudra *symbolises the generative power of the* Lingam, *or Masculine principle.*

THE SECULAR CITY ...
(HOLDING ON TO THE VISION)

All I knew was that you had to run, run, run, without knowing why you were running.

ALAN SILLITOE

If you work with young people today, you may well be struck by how difficult they find it to tune in to the spiritual dimension of their lives. Worse still, you may even be struck by how secular your own life is becoming. Like a creeping paralysis the materialistic gains ground on the divine. Many of us feel threatened by this. Tony de Mello constantly tried to forge useful links between the secular and the divine and he knew it was not easy.

Fr John Main, the Benedictine priest, tried to do the same thing, telling a nice story about a young boy and his old uncle who went out for a walk in their city. Now the city was a very modern one with plenty of delightful buildings and very up-to-date people. It was called Secular City and was beautifully situated in a deep valley with spectacular high mountains rising up all around it. The small boy and his uncle had strayed into the oldest part of town and the young lad was very surprised when their walk took them to a large castle-like building in a ruinous condition. This was a most unusual sight in such a modern city and the young lad wanted to know all about the building and its history. He was particularly interested in one aspect of the building – the remains of a staircase leading to a very large tower – and he wanted to know what it was and how it had got into such a desperate condition. The uncle was reluctant to talk about the ruined tower but finally explained that it had once been the focal point of the building and that it reached high above the Secular City. He also said that it was reputed to have a beautiful view over the whole area. He explained that a special group of people used to live there who did an important job for the community. The Secular City is surrounded by mountains and so people tend to get a bit insular and tend to think of everything in terms of the Secular City. But long ago the group who lived there used to climb up to the high tower and when they saw the view it added a new dimension to the life of the whole community. People could not understand why the monks who lived there were providing schools and hospitals, orphanages and old people's homes for the area. The uncle thought it had something to do with the view from the top of the tower. The climb to the top of the tower was very difficult and as the years went by the stairs became worn and dangerous. Eventually the monks decided they would have to rebuild the stairs and that was when all the trouble started. Some wanted to do a simple repair job, but others wanted to pull down the old tower and build a new one. Some even wanted to install an elevator and the plans became more complex. There had always been some monks at the top of the stairs looking at the view and others on their way up but then the whole group became so involved, they all came down to join in the discussions. It was not long before they began to lose sight of the vision they used to have. Lacking this vision, the monks lost heart in the rebuilding project and now all that remains is a shell. The stairs have disappeared and the monks are gone. Sometimes people remember the monks and their vision, but they are forgotten by most people.

This may well be a parable which has a special meaning for us today. Without the spiritual vision, men and women perish, and the vision cannot be kept alive or developed without time being devoted to prayer and reflection.

Cardinal Basil Hume of Westminster recently spoke in a similar vein about the need to retain vision through prayer. When he speaks about prayer he always manages to throw refreshing light on the subject. He mentions that even though he has to engage daily with a secular culture which can be both sceptical and essentially irreligious he still sticks to what he believes is an essential truth, that we all have a space within us that only God can fill. In western Europe we have squeezed God out of our culture whereas in eastern Europe it was the secular authorities that tried to drive religion out of their society. They didn't succeed, so perhaps we in the west have been the more successful. There is something in the human spirit which is striving always for fundamental meaning about the purpose of life. As regards those who are sceptical and cynical about this, the cardinal asks them to look within themselves and ask the questions: 'What is the purpose of my life and why am I here? What happens after death?'

Cardinal Hume says that St Benedict makes the praise of God the first duty of a monk. When you come to think of it that is a duty that is incumbent of all baptised people. It may be true that monks have a disciplined life with certain times set aside for prayer but it is also true that anyone who wants to be in contact with God has to do something similar – find the time, space and place to pray – for if most people prayed only when they felt like it they wouldn't pray at all. Learning to pray takes discipline. What seems like a burden at the beginning, if persevered with, becomes a delight.

There certainly is a danger today that the secular may swamp the divine. However I see signs of hope in recent events that we may be beginning to wake up to the poverty of the totally secular. Many people question how society is developing and some suggest that we have to go deeper, much deeper, than heretofore in order to rediscover the importance of spirituality. Even the young are sensing this. We need to respond to the intimacy that God wants to have with us. This is the heart of religion and should be what motivates and inspires us.

Today, many people are interested in prayer. They want to know what it is and how they can engage in it. They seek meaning and purpose in their lives. More and more they are beginning to realise that their personal happiness and sense of fulfilment isn't satisfied by the material well-being that may come in consequence of the many goods that are provided by the consumer society. 'Man does not live by bread alone'. There is always a yearning deep in the hearts of people for meaning and purpose. Religion calls for a response to something outside ourselves, that sense of God calling us to return to him, that conversion of the heart for which the Lord came into the world when he said, 'Repent, and believe the gospel'.

Sinead O'Connor, the popular and controversial Irish singer, echoed these views when she spoke to an Irish newspaper in a 1995 interview. 'I consider myself a keener,' she said, 'for I'm a person who makes people cry their grief. Since I was a teenager, I always chopped bits and bits of my hair off, and then I chopped off lumps and lumps, and finally I got to the point of shaving all my hair off, because there was nowhere else to go. What I see is a massive loss of contact with any spirituality. People don't believe in any kind of God. I have the sense that the way to live life is to acknowledge that there is a power greater than ourselves, which can be called upon. Once you lose that, you lose all knowledge of how to live life.' Perhaps we all try to cut off bits of ourselves because we are unable or unwilling to live with the purely secular.

The American philosopher Henry Thoreau wrote, 'Most men live lives of quiet desperation because we are in danger of losing all meaning and purpose in our lives'. Fr Tony de Mello never failed to harp on the same theme. He was particularly fond of telling the story of the inventor who arrived one day in the camp of an ancient tribe. This inventor was a particularly good man, and had just discovered a simple way to make fire. The tribe found fire a particularly important commodity because they needed it to keep warm and to cook their meat. Up to now, they had to hire someone for the sole purpose of lighting fires and the primitive method employed was to rub two stones together until a spark appeared. The inventor's method was altogether simpler. As he was a generous man he showed how they could get a fire going by his new and easier method. The people were delighted for they could see the many advantages of the new method. The only members who did not seem particularly pleased were the priests. They could see that the newly-arrived inventor was winning over the minds and hearts of the people. If this state of affairs continued they would 'lose face' and their hold over the people would be weakened. Thus the priests devised a simple plan. They had the inventor killed, but being fearful of the people they praised the inventor highly and had a shrine built in his memory. Before this shrine they placed a picture of the inventor and they lit small fires to honour the man and his talents. Each day people came to pray at the shrine thanking God for the inventor and his gifts. As the years went by, however, his secret of how to make fire became lost and now all that remained was a grubby relic of the man with a few dying embers placed before it.

Fr Tony de Mello – when he was finished telling this story – used to clap his hands and say, 'What I want to know is, where's the fire?' For him, faith that brings no sense of joy or 'good-news' is a fraud. He knew that life-giving religion is the fire and he feared greatly that we have killed the real thing and have replaced it with a pale substitute.

THE GOOD SAMARITAN
(LUKE 10: 25-37)

For some time I have been fascinated with the power of the imagination. It can, if allowed, unfold much that is true in our inner lives. It can also lead one to Jesus and to a greater awareness of His presence in our lives. So, for this exercise sit comfortably and keep your head upright and your back straight. Quieten yourself by means of one of the breathing exercises. Become aware of your feelings. Take your time and allow the imagination to unfold, revealing the truths stored in the depths of your being.

Now imagine yourself as the poor person set upon by robbers as they make their way through life. For you, who and what is the enemy? Is your enemy one or many? What are the attacks the enemy hurt you with? Are they physical, moral, emotional, psychological? Where and how are you attacked most? How do you react to the pain and weakness you feel?

Now change the focus of your attention to your ordinary living. As you think about real life, what images, thoughts, past memories, hurt feelings, rejections come to mind? After some time begin to think about people who have come to your assistance, like the Good Samaritan, during your life. Feel the care and attention they offered you and allow the strength and energy return to your body because of their goodness. Think of the occasions when Jesus came to your assistance. What were those occasions? What are the wounds you want to be healed of most? What freedom do you ask Jesus to bestow on you? What is your greatest need at the moment? Ask Jesus to heal you and to make you a free person. Listen to anything He may want to say to you. In your own good time end the exercise gently and slowly by using one of the closing exercises. For example, you might listen for the sounds deep within you, becoming aware of the gentle rising and falling of your breath. Then allow your attention to move outwards to the sounds within the room you are praying in. Finish by allowing the focus of your attention to move outwards to any sounds you can hear outside the room you are in.

When the exercise is over, allow yourself some time to mull over what the imagination unfolded before you. If it seems helpful and if you are praying in a group setting, share as much as you wish with a friend or guide.

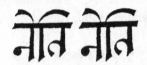

QUIETING EXERCISE

Take up your prayer position and let your body relax. Gently, become aware of your breathing.

Feel the air as it comes in through your nostrils.

Get in touch with the rhythm of your breathing.

As you breathe, feel the touch of the breath as it enters or leaves your body ... test whether it is warm or cold ... listen for its sound ...

Imagine the breath as a coloured fog or candle light and see it in your imagination as it makes its way through your nostrils, hitting the back of your throat, moving down to your shoulders. Continue to visualise it as if you had a glass body, seeing the coloured fog move down to your chest, down your arms, circling around your back-bone, and then see it make its way down to your belly-button area.

After a few moments, again imagine your breath making its return journey back from the pit of your stomach up your back-bone, into your chest, up your arms, to the shoulder area, up to the back of your throat and thence out through your mouth. Now make a prayer of the exercise, choose a mantra and keep repeating the word or phrase as you breathe in and out. You might for example use the word 'Yes' as you breathe in (accepting life from God) and 'Lord' as you breath out (allowing God to take over your life) or you might take a line from one of the Taize chants such as, 'O Lord, hear my prayer, O Lord hear my prayer' on the 'in' breath and follow this with, 'When I call, answer me', on the 'out' breath.

Give this exercise about ten or fifteen minutes and hopefully you will notice that your body begins to become more relaxed. In this way you will allow your imagination to unfold its secrets to you.

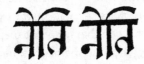

A NOVEMBER MEDITATION

I have used this meditation during the month of November to pray and give thanks for those who have died. I normally start the session by reminding group members that people have died belonging to them who have been very kind and whom they might now like to remember. We pray either 'for' them or 'to' them depending on whether we believe they are already in heaven and can assist us on our journey there or otherwise we think they are in a place of waiting and need our prayers to help them towards their true destiny. I ask all those who have a person in mind to take a candle in their hands which they can use as a symbol and a reminder of their loved one.

I begin the session by using a song of Mary Black's called 'Wonder Child' and I explain that I think of the person I am remembering as a wonderful person who meant so much to me. I ask the participants to close their eyes. It helps greatly if I can recall personally a person that was special to me and tell the group why that person was so special. Then I explain that in my imagination I see my special person – for instance, a deceased Jesuit colleague – making his way upwards towards God as if he were slowly climbing a stony mountain path. Along the way I notice large boulders occasionally placed by the side of the path and I sense that my weary friend is tempted to give up his journey and sink down to rest. This is where my task begins. I pray for the remembered one asking the Lord to encourage and give him strength to complete his task. I know that in due time he will pray for me. I finish the remembrance with the same song as I used at the beginning.

Some cautionary notes. As you might expect, some people can be quite upset when they pray for their loved one in this fashion. I always give group members some idea of the type of session ahead and allow time out for those who feel that the prayer may be too distressing to excuse themselves. I also try to ensure that no one in the group has suffered a very recent bereavement. As a final precaution, I generally try to give group members time after the session to talk over what happened for them, with their neighbour, if they so wish.

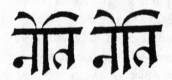

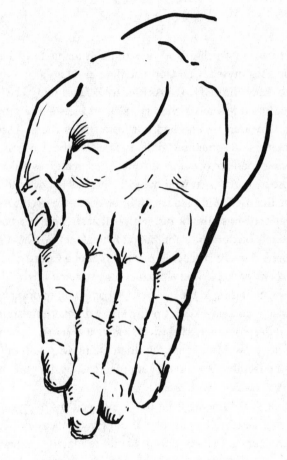

The Abhaya Mudra:
A 'fear-dispelling' posture frequently associated with the Buddha.

PAIN IN OUR WORLD

Death is not extinguishing the light, but putting out the lamp because the dawn has come.

TAGORE

Facing pain in our life is always difficult for us but I have a question for myself. Can God use the pain that occurs in our lives to show Himself to us? As Meister Eckhart said, 'The faithful God often lets his friends fall sick and lets every prop on which they lean be knocked out from under them'. Dietrich Bonhoeffer said something similar: 'I believe that God can and will bring good out of evil, even out of the greatest evil. For that purpose he needs men who make the best use of everything. I believe that God will give us all the strength we need to resist in times of distress. But he never gives that strength in advance, lest we rely on ourselves and not on Him alone'. So does Christ hide behind every crucifix in our lives? Sheila Cassidy, author of *Good Friday People*, and a woman who suffered mightily herself says, 'Suffering in life is a fact. Denying it or ignoring it will not make it go away. I don't really know if it has a meaning or not, but deep down in my heart I believe that it has. This, however, I do know. More important than asking why suffering exists is the fact that we should get in there alongside those who suffer and be there with them'.

Some little time ago the following incident happened to me. I was asked to be part of a Youth Prayer Weekend. These weekends are extremely popular and are mainly arranged in order to help young people with faith development. My task during the weekend was to be available for consultation if anybody wanted to speak to a priest. A short way into the conference three young women came to the door of the consultation room. Two of them linked their reluctant companion between them and sat her down on one of the empty chairs. They then departed. For quite a few minutes there was dead silence but then, slowly, bit by bit, the young woman began to tell her story. We shall call her Aoife and she explained that she had been engaged to be married, but mid-way through the engagement Aoife noticed that the young man she was going out with drank a good deal more than she would have wished. Determined to sort out this problem before it became a major bone of contention between the two of them, Aoife finally insisted that the engagement be postponed and, if her fiancé could stay off drink for a six month period, then they would resume their relationship and go on to be married. If, however, the young man could not manage to stay sober then they should both take it as a sign that they were not suited to each other. After a very few days, the young man came to Aoife saying that he was a reformed character and that he would definitely stay off drink from then on, but that he really wanted them to resume their relationship as the separation was killing him. Aoife, however, insisted that they stick by their agreement and her fiancé went off in a morose state saying he felt so badly he felt like doing away with himself. With tears in her eyes Aoife related how, some hours later, she received a message from the local police asking her to go immediately to her boyfriend's house as he had barricaded himself there and was now threatening to shoot himself. When she managed to get to his house, she discovered that she was just too late. The young man had acted on his threat and had indeed taken his own life.

This whole incident had such a traumatic effect on Aoife that she returned to her own house and, as she put it herself, became a recluse. She would neither eat nor socialise and her future became a matter of indifference to her. For weeks this state of affairs continued and her health began to suffer. Her friends became seriously concerned about her well-being but only one managed finally to break through her shell. Each evening her younger sister returned from school and insisted on coming into her room, where she sat on the bed and recounted all the gossip and news of the day. With little or no encouragement from Aoife, the younger sister continued to keep this action up for months and months finally telling Aoife that she herself was coming to this Youth Weekend and insisting that Aoife come with her. On the weekend itself the younger sister had dragged Aoife along to talk to me. As Aoife herself put it, 'My younger sister gave me back my life, for when God seemed to care for me no longer and I myself had no interest in going on with life, she refused to let me give up'.

As Tony de Mello was fond of pointing out, in each of our lives there are difficulties, hardships, minor disasters or even major tragedies. At such moments God may seem very far away from us.

THERE ARE MANY POSSIBLE reactions to pain as it presents itself in our lives so let us look at a few of our possible responses.

Reaction One. The first reaction may be one of anger. Many of us react with fear to threatening situations in our lives. Quite often we are not sure where the fear comes from or why it should be there at all. It may be grounded in some childhood memory such as the fear of being in someone else's hands, or of not being in control of our own life situations. That vague sense of childish fear may have progressed with us into teenage years because of bullying or peer-pressure. The fear may then have increased as the years rolled on. Will we get fixed up with an unsuitable partner at marriage or with no partner at all? Perhaps our marriage may break-up or we may become unemployed or something may happen to one of our children. Sometimes the fear is a nameless one and we do not even know what terrifies us. If not fought against, this kind of nameless fear can overpower and paralyse us. I recall one person I worked with who regularly dreamed of being alone in a strange house where shapeless ghosts used to follow her around the house tapping the windows and leaving her absolutely terrified. Finally one night in her dream she turned around and faced her fear. In a way she befriended the strange creature, and straightaway, the ghost stopped being terrifying any more. It was as if the simple fact of facing up to the fear within her banished it.

Reaction Two. A second way of reacting to pain in our lives is by being petrified. You may recall how the apostles reacted in the upper room when they realised they had lost their Lord and Master. They were immobilised. The former Soviet Union Party Chairman, Mr Khrushchev, recounts how he responded similarly when threatened. He tells a story of how he had to speak to a packed Presidium in Moscow about the terrors of the Stalinist era and in the very middle of his speech a voice came up from the back of the hall which challenged him and asked, 'Where were you Comrade Khrushchev, when all this terror was taking place. Why didn't you challenge Stalin about the situation whilst he was still alive?' Khrushchev says that he shouted out as loudly as he could that the coward at the back of the hall who had asked the question without revealing himself should stand up. A terrifying silence gripped the hall. No one dared stand up or speak further for fear of the consequences. Then, in the deep silence, Khrushchev quietly whispered, 'I was like you, Comrade. I failed to speak because terror overcame me'.

Third Reaction. The third reaction to painful situations in our lives may be to complain that God is being unfair to us. We may become one of life's complainers. I am reminded here of one of Tony de Mello's stories about a man who wanted to join a very strict religious order. It was explained to him that the rule of the order allowed one to speak to the abbot only once every five years, and then only to say two words. After five years the abbot called up this man and said to him, 'Give me your two words'. The fellow said, 'Terrible food'. Five years later the abbot again called him up and said 'Give me your two words'. The fellow said 'Hard bed'. Five years later, the Abbot again asked the fellow for his two words and he replied, 'Cold room'. Five years after that again the exercise was repeated and this time the fellow said, 'To tell you the truth I'm sick and tired of this place and I have decided to leave'. The abbot then said, 'I'm not a bit surprised, good riddance to you, for you have done nothing but complain since you came here'.

In a similar vein I am reminded of a woman mystic who lived in Baghdad many years ago and who was asked by her followers what was the first step needed to achieve the virtue of acceptance and patience in life. 'Stop complaining', she said. At first her followers were rather disappointed not to be given some more profound and spiritual advice, but somehow the words kept ringing in their ears so that whenever the impulse to complain arose within them they would meditate on her words of wisdom and know that until they stopped complaining, it was a waste of time to think about gaining patience or acceptance.

When Tony de Mello worked with groups he often told them an old Indian story which goes something like this: There was a man who was forever complaining to God about how badly things went for him in his life and finally God could stand the constant string of complaints no longer. He appeared before the man and told him that He would grant three requests to him, but after that God said that He never wanted to hear another depressing request. The man was overjoyed and immediately asked if his wife of many years standing might be allowed die so that he could take on a younger and prettier model. This was done, and the man was overjoyed, but in the days leading up to the funeral a constant stream of friends came up to the man lamenting the great sadness that had come into his life and how he had lost his greatest treasure. 'Just think,' they said, 'how she complemented you and how she put up with all your idiosyncrasies'. When the man realised the truth of their remarks he went running back to God and asked if he could possibly have his wife restored to him. 'Very well,' God said, 'but you do realise that you are using up the second of your three requests'. Well, for a week after that the man made no further requests of God and his silence stretched into a month, and then a year, and finally, after about ten years without a request, the Lord could stand the tension no longer. He went to the man to find out why he had lost his habit of complaining and nagging and the poor man confessed that he could not settle on what he should ask for as his third request. Some of his friends suggested he should ask for money, but others told him such a gift would be useless if he did not have his health. Others counselled that he should ask for a long life and good health, but wiser heads said that if he requested such a gift and did not have happiness in his life, the result would be terrible. And so the man blurted out, 'Lord, could you help me. Could you advise me what I should ask for as my final request'.

The Lord laughed and said to him, 'Ask that you be happy whatever you get'. Wise advice indeed.

Fourth Reaction. A fourth possible response we may have towards facing tragedies in our lives may be a tendency to give up when the going gets tough. Christ himself, in many of His dealings with people in trouble, had to instil courage in His listeners. As He said to the woman at the well, there is a source of spiritual strength within reach, and if you could but see it you would be asking, 'Give me the living water' for that is the surest companion in times of trial.

Fifth Reaction. The fifth reaction towards painful situations in our lives may be a feeling of powerlessness – we can do little

93

about the pain or its cause. Some years ago I was part of the counselling team in a retreat centre where Alcoholics Anonymous weekends were regularly held. I think it can safely be said that those giving the weekends considered it a privilege and a pleasure to be there for they believed that they learned at least as much from the proceedings as did the alcoholics themselves. Those who suffered from this affliction taught us a great deal because they were some of the most honest and courageous people I have ever come across. The first lesson they taught us was that before any recovery could take place, the addicts had to admit certain home truths about themselves. They had to admit that they had failed, that they were sinners, that they could not overcome their frailties by their own strength alone and that, as St Paul said, the very practices they abhorred and wished to discontinue they found themselves falling into time and time again. Something or someone outside themselves was needed if they were to change. 'Who will rescue me?' had to be their constant cry and they realised that some form of higher power was their only chance. They needed to go to the well for the 'living water', so that, as St Paul might say, having lost everything they might then regain their self-respect and come to believe the words of Christ, 'My grace is sufficient for you'.

In the lives of many people there comes a time of total loss. Perhaps they get sick or depressed. They may suffer the loss of dear ones, their job, their financial security, or their peace of mind. Friends may desert them or they may even lose whatever good name or reputation they had in former times. Cardinal Joseph Bernardin of Chicago found himself in just such a nightmare situation when he was accused of sexual misconduct in November 1993 and was sued for ten million dollars. His own words sum up his dilemma and despair. 'My feeling was one of disbelief and bewilderment, and then my mood turned to anger, and after that to compassion and sorrow for my accuser. That is where I am now'. Imagine the scene. A lawsuit had been taken out against the cardinal by a thirty-four year old man who suffered from AIDS and it referred to one episode of molestation, said to have taken place about twenty year before between 1975 and 1977. The newspapers and television reports splashed the headlines across the world and suggested that the charges must be grounded in some sort of reality. Then came the second bomb-shell. The AIDS victim revealed that the story and accusation were not true and that they arose from false and unreliable memories induced through hypnosis. Afterwards, Cardinal Bernardin said that the months surrounding the accusations were like a waking nightmare. We can imagine how he felt humiliated by the public attack on his character and the feelings of powerlessness which must have been present. There were few enough sensible ways to refute such a charge. The darkness did not overcome him, however, and afterwards he was able to point to some areas of growth which he himself felt as a result of the crisis. 'It had a powerful spiritual impact on me,' he said, 'and I have a tremendous sympathy for anyone who has been falsely accused'. The cardinal also made it his business not to let the nightmare overwhelm him. He decided to contact his accuser and visit him in hospital. The young man wanted to meet with the cardinal to apologise for the embarrassment and hurt he had caused. Because the words used during their interaction were simple, direct and deeply moving, the meeting, in the cardinal's own words was 'a grace-filled one which brought closure and peace to both of us'.

WHAT MIGHT ONE DO to extract light out of the darkest moments that befall us in our lives? The following suggestions may be useful. One possible thing to do is to just sit down and be quiet. Look at how we respond to painful situations and work out what are the causes behind that response. By doing that we may begin to recognise that our response is an angry or fearful one and in that case we might pray that God will change our mind-set.

Many courageous people, faced with fearful situations in life, suggest that a pro-active or fighting response is necessary. Brian Keenan, Terry Waite and Sheila Cassidy are examples of people who have faced life-threatening and potentially soul-destroying situations in the recent past. Their comments about how they dealt with their horrifying ordeals are illuminating. They summed up their response with the phrase, 'You may break my body but you will not break my spirit'. They refused to allow the disasters of the present moment to overwhelm them. They used any tactic to dispel fear. One wrote down in book form the incidents and horrors that were happening. Another painted the scenes in picture form, and the third went to the sea shore and roared out his pain and grief to the waves. All tried to pour themselves into the present moment and refused to think either of the fears that had gone before or of those that might arise in the future. All knew that it is better to bring fear out into the open rather than hold it inside where it might implode. They knew that grief or pain could be treated as a gift or threat in life and that it might be in our frailty, not in our power, that we find Christ.

Let us end our reflections on dealing with pain in our life with the story of King Saul in the Old Testament. You may recall that King Saul was very down-hearted and distressed at one point in his life and on the advice of his counsellors he decided to arrange a banquet to cheer himself up. In order that music might be provided for the occasion, he arranged that his woodcutters should be sent out to the royal forests to saw down oak-trees to make a special harp. He then sent other tradesmen into his workshops to manufacture strings for the harp. At last, the night of the banquet arrived. At the height of the festivities the new harp was wheeled out to centre stage. As soon as the harp player plucked the first string, disaster struck. No sound came forth from the instrument. Experts were brought from all over the court to explain why this should be so, but none could give a reason. Still less could they make the instrument play. Finally one expert suggested that the boy, David, should be brought to the palace to see if he could throw any light on the matter. When David arrived he sat down and gently put his ear beside the strings of the harp. He waited for some minutes in that position and then proceeded to bring forth beautiful music from the instrument. When the king asked David afterwards to explain what had been happening, the lad said that he first had to listen and let the harp tell its story. It told David how it had started life as a tiny acorn before becoming a giant oak in the forest. It explained how it had withstood the hardships of winter weather, how it had been chopped down and how its strings had been tempered in the white heat of the forge. Only when it had been listened to and revealed the pain of its birth and life could it fulfil its destiny and potential. In a similar way we need to listen to our own life story and see the part pain has played in it.

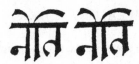

PRODIGAL SON MEDITATION

Having settled yourself into a prayerful position by means of one of the preparatory exercises, I invite you to recall the famous story of the Prodigal Son from St Luke's gospel. Place yourself at the scene and go to the father's farmhouse on the night of his son's return. Picture the celebration. Look in through the window at the party going on inside. See the son and the father as they dance around the centre of the floor clapping their hands in celebration. Note their joy and remain with them as the night begins to come to completion. When all have retired, go to the prodigal's room and knock at the door. He won't be asleep. His eyes will be shining. Ask him to tell you his story. Why did he leave home? What were his adventures along the way and why did he decide to come home? How did he feel when he saw his father running down the road to meet him? What were his thoughts when he heard the orders being given to bring out the best robe and ring? And what of the elder brother? How were the two getting along now?

The prodigal will want to tell you what a wonderful change took place in his heart. As he tells the story, remember it is our Father that he is describing. If the father can show such love and interest to the prodigal, perhaps my Father is also showing these things to me?

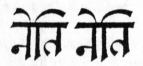

BREATH MANTRA

Take the phrase 'Into your hands, Lord, I commend my spirit' and use it in mantra form. As you breathe in say, 'Into your hands Lord' and allow your breath to match the speed of the phrase. As you breathe out, focus your attention on the exhalation and match the second half of the sentence, 'I commend my spirit', to the natural rhythm of your release of air. Finally, bring the breathing in and breathing out phrases together as you inhale and exhale with the full phrase. Let the sentence sink in to your being slowly, almost as if water were soaking in to parched and rocky ground.

HANDS MEDITATION

Put in simple terms, meditation may be described as the process of relaxing my body and mind so that I can quietly go within myself. I try first to find a body posture which focuses my mind and keeps me alert. The posture should create few pressure points on my body but should not be so relaxed that it induces sleep. The aim of meditation is to remain present to both myself and my God. If I am using a sitting position, it should be on a straight-backed chair and my feet should be firmly planted on the floor. I place my hands in my lap with the palms up. I note my breath pace, and because breathing can be related to physical well-being, I try to keep it slow and regular. As I mentioned before, when we are stressed and tense our breathing becomes erratic, taut, shallow or irregular for our body knows our state of mind.

Now start the prayer exercise.

Look down at your hands and imagine them as they were when you were a child. Reflect on how much you needed at that stage and how others had to do virtually everything for you. Call to mind those who took on the bulk of this caring and call down a blessing on them. Now conjure up an image of those who cared for you in moments of need and place their intentions before the Lord. When you feel ready, try to imagine those who will look after you in future needy times such as times of sickness and old age and send a blessing for them on ahead of you.

Now think of those who needed your hands on different occasions: those who needed you in moments of pain and those who needed your hands to bless, comfort or hold them.

Finally cast your mind forward and pray for those who may need your hands in the future. Ask that the hands you see before you may be given the strength to be equal to the task.

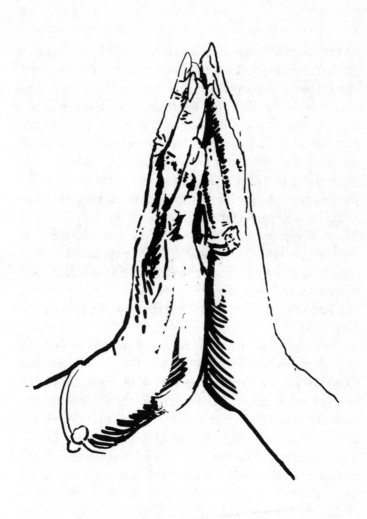

FINDING THE GAIN IN PAIN

Pain is whatever the patient says hurts.

AN IRISH DOCTOR

As I sit down to write this I have just come in from bringing a fifteen-year-old to the hospital after she had taken an overdose. The girl has been through a great deal over the past six months with both her mother and father dying of tragic illnesses. Recently, affairs in her life have come to a head and the pain and hurt of her aloneness have become more and more apparent to her. Now they have become almost unbearable and her action today of taking a fistful of tablets seems like an easier way out than working her way through the distress. The overriding message coming through to those in contact with her is, 'I cannot keep my life in focus much longer and I have to do something to relieve the anguish'. C. S. Lewis puts it another way. 'Pain insists on being attended to'. He says that 'God whispers to us in our pleasures, speaks to us in our conscience, but shouts to us in our pain for it is His megaphone to rouse a deaf world'.

So some pain, if it is to be growthful, has to be gone through and understood. As Our Lady did in her life, we may have to be patient with pain, storing it in our hearts, to see if it can teach us anything in its allotted time. It may be beneficial to leave the ache undisturbed until the time seems ripe, lest any attempt at removal should do untold damage. As an example you might think of the man in the gospel story who attempted to drive a devil out of his house. He swept his establishment and indeed succeeded in clearing the devil out, only to find that by disturbing one difficulty he had created many more. His one devil had been replaced by seven more in the space he had created. I can perhaps describe this situation more clearly by outlining a scenario from my own life. I drive a motor-bike and recently found that a large ugly nail had lodged itself in my front tyre. As I was many miles from the nearest repair-shop, I had to leave the nail in place, despite the risk, knowing that at least the nail itself was keeping some air in the tyre. If I had removed the nail too quickly, the end result would have been much more troublesome than my initial problem. So sometimes, one must leave the pain in place until the time and circumstances are right to effect a repair.

The saints themselves often had to be patient with their pain. Many of them had a 'desert' or harrowing experience in their lives and St Teresa of Avila speaks frequently of this and gives thanks for the suffering she had to endure in her life and the ability she found within herself to draw fruit from that suffering.

Pain, as well as being something we have to attend to, can also, in special circumstances, be something of a gift. How so? The pain or distress may give prior warning of difficulties ahead. It may alert us to weaknesses in the body or the spirit that need to be cured. As with any injury, healing occurs not just when two edges of a wound come together. That factor only allows the individual to carry on as before. More significant is when the healed ones realise that a change of behaviour in their lives is now necessary if they are to remain healthy in the future. When I talk about pain or distress here I mean any kind of suffering, confusion, alienation, fear, or brokenness. One often notices that those who have been through great pain themselves are deep and caring individuals. One suspects they have been somehow deepened because of their pain. A type of spirituality seems to permeate through them making them more able listeners and more considerate empathisers. Almost without their knowing it, they seek a strength beyond their own. This deepening of the spirit doesn't necessarily come about in some sudden burst of insight. More usually it is a piecemeal development and may be so gradual that for many people it is unperceived, unrealised and often unused. This fact was pointed out to me during a workshop given by a doctor who spent all his time in hospitals working with those in the last stages of life. The speaker was a wonderful man and any observations he had about working with those in pain were well worth hearing. When I asked him if dealing with those who were about to die, telling them the truth about their illnesses and listening to their cry for help was tremendously draining, his answer was crystal clear: 'No, because I don't really tell the patients how they are, they tell me'. He went on to explain that when patients came to the hospital to begin their final journey, he normally took some time before he introduced himself to them. He began the interview by asking them to outline their own understanding of their illness. After this he just sat back and listened to their replies. 'People guide you by their answers,' he said, 'and shape for you what they themselves are able to hear. If they say they are feeling very well, I nod in agreement and say how delighted I am. These people are telling me they are not yet ready within themselves to receive any more distressing news for the present. However, other patients say to me straight away that they do not think they are very well at all. I agree. I do not want to lie to them. They have shown themselves ready for the truth. In fact they have faced the truth head-on themselves'.

All of us have to deal with pain and distress at some time in our lives, whether it be of a spiritual, mental, emotional, social or physical variety. At such times it is difficult to remember that the pain we are experiencing may be beneficial. It seldom feels so at the time. The pain may be telling us something. It may be highlighting the fact that something is radically wrong with us and that we had better do something about it. Tony de Mello noted that when we work with our own pain timing is vital. The time and circumstances must be ripe. If we hold off and do nothing, disaster may result. Similarly, if we rush in too quickly, the result may be calamitous. To illustrate this point, De Mello told a nice story about Zorba the Greek: Zorba remembered one morning when he discovered a cocoon in the bark of a tree, just when the butterfly was making a hole in its case and getting ready to come out. Zorba waited but he thought the butterfly was very slow. He was impatient so he bent over the cocoon and breathed on it to heat it as quickly as he could and then a miracle happened. The case opened and the trembling butterfly tried to unfold its wings. Zorba tried to help it with his breath. But it needed to be hatched out slowly and the unfolding of the wings should have been a gradual process in the sun. Now it was too late. Zorba's breath had forced the butterfly to appear before its time. It struggled desperately to survive but, having been forced beyond its natural pace, it died in the palm of his hand. When Zorba told the story aftwards he said that the tiny butterfly as the greatest weight he had on his conscience. He felt it was a mortal sin to violate the great laws of nature. As he said: 'We should not hurry, we should not be impatient, but we should confidently obey the eternal rhythm'.

Let things happen at their own pace. So it is with pain. Some pain has to be let take its course if it is to bear fruit. The pain may colour all subsequent events in our lives and ensure that future happenings bring with them the potential they contain. As C. S. Lewis said, 'The pain then is part of the happiness now'.

Other types of pain or envy in life have to be let go if they are not to destroy us. To illustrate this point, I particularly like Tony de Mello's story about two monks who set out from their monastery on a long day's pilgrimage. The two had only just set out when they came to a river in full flood which was obviously not going to be easy to cross. Standing at the side river, obviously hoping to get across, was a delightful-looking young woman. They first monk never gave her a glance but plunged into the water and made his way to the other side with difficulty. The second monk, being of a different ilk, pinned up his habit and put the young woman up on his shoulders. Braving the current, and at considerable risk to his own life, he managed to carry the girl safely to the far bank, where he deposited her before joining his companion on their journey. For most of that day, the two monks trudged along together in silence. The first monk had a countenance that was as black as thunder, whereas the one who had carried the woman across the river seemed in very good spirits. When the two finally sat down for lunch, the bad-humoured monk began to give out to his companion saying that he could not possibly see how a monk with a vow of chastity could have left himself so open to temptation by hoisting such an attractive young woman up on his shoulders. His partner simply replied, 'I left her at the river bank'. Enough said. One had done what was needed to be done and had then got on with his task. The other monk had carried the image, envy and frustration of the happening with him throughout the day. So some pains, if carried unnecessarily, fester and damage. Reflection, prayer, and a simple request to the Lord may mean that we become finer persons having gone through sickness or pain.

Tony de Mello looked at questions of pain, illness and healing, time after time in his workshops. In his first Irish retreat and also in his first book *Sadhana* he brought us back to the gospel story of the man at the pool in Siloh. On both occasions he reflected on the story and posed a difficult question. Let me recall the gospel scene first. You will remember that near Jerusalem there was a famous holy healing spot known as the Pool of Siloh. Basically, this was a sort of watering hole surrounded by steps where pilgrims used to gather each day in the hope of obtaining a cure. Tradition had it that an angel of the Lord would occasionally appear beside the pool and wave a wand over the waters, making them move. The first person who managed to get into the water after the waters moved would be cured. Now the gospels tell us that one man had been going to the pool-side each day for thirty-eight years. The question Tony de Mello placed before us during his first Irish workshop was, 'Do you think the sick man wanted to be cured?' I think I was the youngest Irish Jesuit present on that occasion – certainly I was the most naive – and I still recall how incredulous I was at his question. I think I put up my hand and blurted out my answer. 'Of course the man wanted to be cured. Sure why would he have come to the pool for thirty-eight years otherwise?'

Tony de Mello replied with a smile. 'If you think that, you don't know too much about human nature'.

He then asked us to imagine the scene for ourselves. The sick man was paralysed so he must have had friends who carried him down to the pool each day. Probably he had a wife who made his lunch for him before he set out. In all probability he received great sympathy from those around the pool who knew his story and knew also how long he had been coming to this place. If he was really determined to have himself cured, he would surely have managed to get himself a pool-side seat after so many years to ensure the success of his mission, but this he failed to do.

Then De Mello asked us to conjure up a picture of the day Jesus came to that place and posed His question to the paralysed man: 'Do you want to be healed?' Imagine the questions that must have been going through the poor man's mind. Suddenly the realisation of what he would have to give up if he was given a cure must have dawned on him. No longer would his friends fetch and carry for him. His wife would cease the lunch-making and insist that he go out and get himself a job. Even his best friends would begin to view him in a new and envious light. Their expectations of what he might achieve in life would be raised. As De Mello himself said, 'I'd say the man thought twice before he said yes to a cure. He could so easily have decided that after all he didn't want to be cured. The price was just too high'. Is it the same for us? Do we really want to bear the pain in order that the fruit beyond it may appear?

One last point before we leave the question of working with pain in our lives. Some years ago I was invited to attend an Easter Saturday night liturgy in a northern Ireland study centre. I remember driving up to the college very late on that Holy Saturday night and finding some of the students who had decided to stay up all night. They were in the coffee room. The Easter Mass was scheduled for six o'clock the following morning. It had been decided that the ceremony would take place outdoors on a local mountain-side. Shortly before the event, we all began to get into our rain-gear and followed the celebrant into the freezing darkness. In single file we made our way along a hilly track that led to the summit. When we reached the allotted spot, we could just make out the outline of Carlingford Lough beneath us and on the hilltop itself, the shape of a large unlit bonfire was evident. The preacher began his sermon by asking us to recall the pain and loneliness of Lent which we had just been through. Then he came to the climax of his talk. Taking as his final line an ancient Irish proverb, he took a burning torch and held it to the bonfire twigs. Three things then happened simultaneously. The bonfire – symbol of Easter hope – shot flames into the sky. At the same moment, the first streak of morning light crept across the night sky, and simultaneously a bird began to sing the first notes of day. The Irish proverb used was: 'If you keep a green branch alive in your heart in the hour of darkness, then the Lord will come and send a bird to sing from that branch with the dawning of the day'. Perhaps we too can have patience with the painful moments in our lives so that the Lord, in His own time, may send the bird to sing for us and make those experiences fruitful.

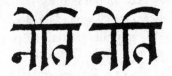

THE MOUNTAINSIDE

Theme – to find out what our instinctive reaction to pain is.

With this exercise you have to use great discretion. It may be inappropriate for you at this time to reflect upon the painful areas of your life. If it seems valuable, examine patterns in your life as you recall past experiences.

Preparatory Exercise. Close your eyes and become aware of your breathing. Allow your breath to still you. Zone in on what you are feeling in your body at this moment. Make yourself comfortable and if you feel a particular tension in any part of your body just register that. When you have got some sense of what you are feeling in your body and what is going on within you, quietly bring those feelings to the Lord and ask Him to give you wholeness through His grace. This meditation is about storms and troubles in your life.

Imagine you are waiting for an elevator on the fifth floor of a building.

The elevator arrives ... this is a different type of elevator. It does not take you to the bottom of a building but to the bottom of your innermost self.

You enter the elevator on the fifth floor ... the door closes and you start going down. As you descend from the fifth floor a sense of wonder fills your mind for you may never have been in this place before. You move down to the fourth floor and you are filled with a sense of mystery, because you are not sure what you will find. Now you go down to the third floor and the excitement grows as you anticipate what you may find. Now travel down to the second floor and the quietness grows. The lift goes down to the bottom floor and the door of the lift opens. You step out onto the ground floor and what you see amazes you.

You are on the side of a high mountain and you find that you have come to this place to take time out and reflect on what has been going on within you. You are going to camp out for the night. It is a warm summer's night and the reason you are all alone is that your expected camping partners have taken a different option than you. They think a storm is coming and have decided to sleep inside a deserted cabin nearby, but you have decided to remain outside. Set up tent. Lie there in your sleeping-bag and look out across the valley towards the lights of a distant town. It is a peaceful sight. Soon you grow tired and begin to fall asleep. Suddenly you awaken with a start. Thunder and lightning are everywhere. Strangely enough, you are not afraid. You feel protected by God. You think back over the past year in your life and reflect on what you have learnt about yourself from living with your family or community. You ask yourself the following questions:

– What challenged me during the past months?
– What did I learn about myself from my family or community?
– What areas within myself need to grow?
– Did I spot any blind spots within myself?
– What were my gifts in community or within my family?
– What gave me life?
– What deadened me over the past months?
– What were the low points?
– What were the high points?

110

- What have I not resolved?
- What do I wish I'd done differently?
- What am I glad I did?
- Were we, or could we have been, Christ for each other as the early Christian community was?

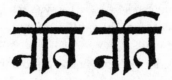

ST PETER IN JAIL
(ACTS OF THE APOSTLES 12:6)

Read the passage first.

Visit St Peter in his cell. Be with him as he looks back on his call. Reflect with St Peter as he thinks out how would life have been for him if he had not responded to Christ's invitation to follow the Christian path.

Now look back on your own life.

- What has been your call?
- Have you followed it?
- Where has it led you?
- Are you happy with your response?
- Do you need to do anything now to make the call more fulfilling?
- What has influenced you?
- Has it been status, money, comfort, a job, or acceptance by others?

Finish up by giving thanks to the Lord for your call.

HEALING OF MEMORIES
(BATTLEGROUNDS REVISITED)

Take a few big sighs, like sighs of relief ... now pay attention to the natural rhythm of your breathing ... feel your body relax as you breathe in and breath out ... with each 'out' breath notice a little more how you can let go ... when you take the 'in' breath notice the feelings of warmth, comfort, stillness, and peace that are present within you ...

Now go back to the store-house of your memories and bring back a memory of a peaceful, magical place from your own childhood, a secret place, just as it was or as you would have liked it to be ... whether it existed or not in reality you have the power to create it now and place it in your imagination. So go back now in memory to picture yourself as a child ... this is the divine core of your being ... take a good look at your child self.

So check ... how old are you ...? how do you look ...? are you happy ...? see within this beautiful child ... it may have been a long time since the child has felt noticed and loved by you in this way ... you may recall some times when you failed to be loving and affirming towards that child self ... look towards that child self and let the child know the beauty you see ... ask to be forgiven for the times you failed to notice the beauty and the times you failed to be gentle and loving towards yourself ... it may be a long time since you noticed or thought about that inner child and there may be many things to tell – perhaps the events of an entire lifetime – the joys, the sorrows, the experiences along the way through which you gained wisdom ... there may be experiences which are still weighing on your heart ... so let the child tell you of such events in words, pictures, feelings, or whatever ... just listen now and be there for that child without any judgement ... do not worry about what has been gone through, what may have been done or undone ...

Now let your childhood self take you by the hand and lead you through a sunlit meadow ... with total innocence the child wants to introduce you to the beauty of the sun, the gentle wind on your face ... wants to take you to a secret place where there is a secret gift for you ... a gift that will help you on your way through this life-time ...

When you come to this secret place, there is a treasure chest, and when it is opened your gift is inside ... what is it? ... you can ask the child about it and the answer may have more wisdom for you ...

Now thank the child, the eternal divine child that dwells forever within you ... know in your heart that as you can never leave that child, it can never leave you, and if you are afraid of forgetting about your inner child take a mental snapshot of the scene now which you can recall whenever you need to ... Bring the session to an end by returning to the place you are in, here and now ... taking your time and enjoying the feelings of companionship ...

In your own time open your eyes.

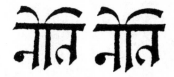

Young People and the Church

Hell is human life stripped without wonder.

Brendan Kennelly

Metropolitan Bloom, leader of the Russian Orthodox Church in Britain, tells a nice story against himself about his very early days as a parish curate. On his first Christmas in a London parish, a little old lady came up to him and asked his advice about prayer and praying. Being raw and shy himself, Archbishop Bloom suggested that the old woman should speak with an elderly and experienced older priest who lived nearby and who was reputed to be an expert on the subject. However the old woman replied, 'For many years I have had detailed conversations with people who are supposed to know something about prayer, but they have never given me a sensible reply to my questions so I thought that as you probably know nothing about the subject you might, by chance, blunder out something useful and point me in the right direction'. The archbishop says he asked the old lady what exactly was her prayer problem and she told him that for fourteen years she had been praying almost continuously and she didn't really seem any closer to God now than when she had started. I think the archbishop finished his story by saying that if she stopped praying continuously for a while, and tried a bit of listening instead, the Lord might be so surprised that he would send her down a few insights.

Sister Wendy, who has recently become famous for her television programmes which look at the beauty of art, recounted a somewhat similar story in her excellent booklet, *Simple Prayer*. She tells of how a famous Jesuit, whilst preaching in St Patrick's Cathedral, New York, was asked by one of his listeners how he managed to make so much out of the topic of prayer because 'prayer is the simplest thing out'. As Sister Wendy recounted the story she added, 'I hope the famous Jesuit did know that, because some of us talk a great deal about prayer but I suspect many of us would rather talk about the subject than actually engage in it'.

I am reminded of these two stories because it seems to me that many young people today are struggling to find some purpose within their lives and the model of Church they are being presented with is at best somewhat tepid and at worst completely meaningless to them. The salt has lost its saltiness. The living water has become stagnant and no longer quenches their thirst. Many older Christians realise this or have some vague sense that something has gone wrong but, despite their best intentions, they feel powerless when it comes to offering practical assistance to youth. They do not know what, if anything, they might helpfully do. They sense that the fire of faith they were brought up with no longer burns brightly. Only a few faintly glowing embers survive. The young people they meet seem to find themselves either unloved and unlovable before God or else they are completely uninterested in the subject.

They remind one of the ugly duckling from Hans Andersen's fairy-tale. You may remember the tale. On a certain farm a duck hatched out a new family of ducklings but as soon as they were born one of the new family was discovered to be considerably larger than the others. The unusual bird did not have the soft golden feathers of the others but was rather dirty and grey in colour. Also it was clumsy and misshapen and was generally the laughing-stock of the farmyard, being jeered at and mocked by the other animals. Life became so unbearable for the ugly duckling that it ran away. After some time it reached a lake in the forest but even there the wild ducks did not want to associate with it. Months passed and the unusual bird grew larger and more ashamed of itself. Winter came and one day it saw three large, beautiful white swans flying over the lake and trees. While admiring their beauty and power of flight the duckling thought to itself, 'If only I could be like them'. Spring came. The ice on the lake melted. Again he saw the three wild swans flying overhead but this time they landed on the lake. He tried to conceal himself because he was afraid of the mockery which he expected would come from such beautiful creatures, but after a short time they called him over to join them. 'I cannot for I'm only an ugly duckling and you would do me a kindness by killing me and putting me out of my misery,' he replied. But they said to him, 'look at your reflection in the water. You are beautiful, you are one of us. You are a swan and can fly high with us'. With a heart bursting with joy, the swan flew over and joined his true family.

How can this sense of their own self-worth be given to young people today? Throughout the gospels we find Christ raising people from their knees and instilling in them a sense of their own beauty. But this sense comes only slowly, possibly in the ordinary, undramatic living out of the slow river of everyday life. Often the sense of self-worth is bestowed on us by our peers or those we associate with. They say that before the slave-trade was abolished Abraham Lincoln was present at a slave market watching the proceedings when a young Negro woman was put on the block to be auctioned. Lincoln joined the bidding – much to the surprise of the onlookers – for his views on slavery were well known. What is more, he managed to outbid the other onlookers who were present and thus became the owner of the slave. He paid the asking price and received the slave papers. Then the unexpected happened. Lincoln went over to the woman and pressed the ownership papers into her hands. 'Take these. Now you are free,' he said. As the woman took the papers guaranteeing her freedom, it dawned on her what this stranger had done. She looked at Abraham Lincoln and asked,

'Does this mean I can go where I like and do what I want?'

'It does,' Lincoln answered.

'Then sir,' the woman said, 'I would like to go with you and serve you for the rest of my life.'

The question that springs readily to mind is, 'Who today can give youth a sense that they have been redeemed by Christ's sacrifice and explain that their freedom has been restored to them?'

Many parents and clergy I meet wish to do this but feel unequal to the task. A partial answer may have been given to me when I recently witnessed a flock of geese flying in to Irish shores from Iceland. An onlooker told me how these geese made their journey. He explained how the flock could only reach their destination if the group members helped each other. He told me how the flock always flew in a characteristic V-shaped formation. If each bird maintained its correct position in the V-shape, an air uplift was created. This helped each bird in the flock to prosper. If any bird got out of line, the others immediately began to feel the extra drag and strain of flight. Always the strongest bird took the lead for as long as it possibly could and when it could no longer maintain the necessary group speed it took up the rearmost position but continued to honk its encouragement from behind, encouraging those in the front to keep up speed. If any bird began to weaken, it dropped out of the group, so that all should not suffer on its behalf, but even then two other birds stayed behind with it to offer protection and hope. When the weak one regained its strength, all three carried on together and tried to regroup with the main bunch. All knew that the strong would side with the weak in difficult times as well as good, in times of weakness as well as strength. Perhaps, in faith terms, young people themselves – through peer ministry – may be the greatest handers-on of the faith to their own generation. Certainly some of them realise that what is being offered to them by today's world is bread that does not ultimately satisfy.

In recent years a sense of despair seems to have set in among some older Christians as they see the young hopelessly adopting the values of modern culture. 'Why don't they see the shallowness?' many ask. The Churches today must be among the few organisations who blame the customer because they do not see the value of the goods they offer. Many young people are searching and striving for a space away from the noise and bustle where they can obtain a central point of stillness within their lives. They have some vague sense that, just as a cart-wheel, if it is not properly balanced, tends to put any vehicle it is connected with out of kilter, so too their own lives, without a purpose, will ultimately lead nowhere. They have caught glimpses of the fact that knowing you are loved is a vital ingredient towards a feeling of self-worth. As the Pope's favourite theologian, Von Balthasar has said, 'If you want to understand faith, just pause for a moment and reflect about something that happened to you when you were about two months old. At that stage in our lives we were loved, we knew we were loved and being loved was what we needed to get us started on the road to growth'. Von Balthasar says that faith is the smile that recognises love. To recognise that smile takes time and stillness. The impetus that gets us going, the starting point, may be a felt desire for quiet, stillness, or what I might call a 'desert' experience.

What is this 'desert' experience and how might we open ourselves to it? Tony de Mello tells a story about a Dutch Jesuit who went to meet his local bishop. When he arrived at the bishop's house he found that the man was away for nine days making his retreat. Locals said he had taken the time to live 'under the sky'. The bishop just dug a hole in the sand with his hands and squeezed himself into it to escape from the breeze. He spent the time there exposed to the elements and to God, knowing that the aloneness of the desert would bring him face to face with God. De Mello finished by saying, 'Don't fail to stop at the desert for the desert has a tremendous attracting power and sucks people in with its stillness'. Many people today question the value of a desert experience. They wonder about the worth and significance of taking time out for prayer. That's precisely what's wrong with us today. We do not see the relevance or value of taking time out. We will spend hours or months or years cultivating our brains. People see that as being perfectly normal and relevant. Tell them however that you intend spending time cultivating your inner spirit and they just don't recognise that there is such a thing. We forget that there is a dimension within us – the spiritual dimension – that clamours for advancement as much as our intellect sphere. Finding and staying with that dimension can be painful. The desert has a nasty habit of turning up areas in our lives that we may not wish to face. It also, however, may give us the breathing-space we need to focus ourselves and turn our lives in the direction that is most healthy for us. That direction is inwards, not outwards.

If we reach for happiness and place our well-being and fulfilment in anything outside ourselves we will be frustrated. Likewise, if we seek our happiness only in people, relationships, money, success or acclaim, we may well find that they are riches that quickly pall. As Creation said to Augustine when he searched for happiness, 'We are not the God you seek. God is he who made us. You must seek beyond us', or as Dag Hammarskjold said, 'We are good at exploring outer space but poor at exploring inner space'. So explore the inner space. It is more difficult but ultimately more satisfying. It may provide a sense of purpose in our lives, purpose which gives life a deep meaning, energises, enthuses and enables us to keep moving ahead. People find this vital, intangible entity in many ways. In the love of and for their children, in the service of others, in creating something original or beautiful. But nearly always, a meaning in life is caught up in love of another.

Recently, I asked a number of young people where they find meaning and purpose in life. Their replies were illuminating. Direct references to God were rarely made. However, many of those questioned caught a glimpse of God in the beauty of the outdoors, looking at nature, sunsets, flowers, babies, animals, or in just walking alone. A few used the words of Brendan Behan, the noted Irish playwright, and said they felt themselves to be 'night-time' Catholics – that is they only prayed when they were in the dark. The above-mentioned places – along with the desert – may be some of the spots where young people can experience the presence of God in their lives. There is one other place and it is illustrated well in a popular African fable.

Two brothers wanted to go to a distant country to make their fortunes and before setting out they asked their father for a blessing. This was given but the father suggested the boys leave their marks along the route they passed on their journey lest they get lost on the way home. The older brother set out and made marks on trees as he journeyed along. The younger brother took another road and dropped in on many of the houses along his route, making friends with the children and the families he encountered. Finally, the two brothers arrived home where they were greeted by their father. He wanted to see the marks the boys had made during their travels. The older brother showed his father all sorts of marks he had made on trees as he made his way along. The two travelled a long distance without eating on their trip. Finally, they returned home empty-handed. When the father set out with his second-born son, the two were warmly welcomed by different friends in the houses which the boy had earlier visited. They were treated as special guests in each place they stopped. Goats were slaughtered to welcome them. They were very happy. They brought home many gifts, including meat and other presents. Then the father summoned his two sons and said: 'Dear sons, I have seen the work that you have done. I will arrange a marriage for the one who has done better'. He turned to the first-born and said, 'My son, I think you are foolish. You did not take care of people. You really made no mark of value'. To the younger son he said, 'You have made good and lasting marks wherever you went'.

So young people may be given a sense of God through the people and peers they encounter along the way. They may be gifted with the insight of D. H. Lawrence who said, 'Man has little needs and deeper needs'. We have fallen into the mistake of living for our little needs. We have almost lost the sense that deeper needs may exist within us. Characters from literature, as well as faith figures, may help return us to the true path. Saul Bellow, in his book, *Henderson, the Rain King*, presents us with the character Henderson who has an inner voice within him which cries out incessantly, 'I want, I want' but the voice would never tell him what it wanted. St Augustine pointed out what that want might be, 'You have made us for Yourself and our hearts are restless until they find their rest in You'. Perhaps Christ Himself gave us the fullest answer, 'Anyone who refuses to believe in the Son will never see life' (John 3:35).

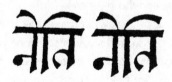

Take up a position which keeps the head and spine erect ... the bodily circuit closed ... and the whole body at once both poised and alert, yet relaxed and comfortable.

The eyes should be closed or half closed. If half closed they should be fixed on a chosen object such as a candle flame or crucifix. The hands should be folded in the lap. Some people find it helpful to meditate while walking. I like this, but remember that whilst it is true that monastic cloisters were built for this purpose it is doubtful if complete abstraction can be obtained whilst the body is moving.

First, concentrate on your breathing because it quietens the body and helps the concentration. It also develops one's inner strength. Now fill the body with air to its maximum capacity and then empty it as far as possible. Begin to breathe, slowly and deeply, with lips slightly open, inhaling through the nose and exhaling through the mouth. Count the breaths, thinking of nothing save the counting. Think of the mind as a pool, whose surface, when ruffled by the winds of anger or desire, is unable to reflect the sun. You are trying to find an interior reflection of God's goodness in your life.

Now begin the meditation. Call to mind some people of your acquaintance who have very little of the world's goods and still seem happy. Ask what makes them happy? You might think of a character from history or someone you have heard or read about recently. Perhaps someone like Brian Keenan or Terry Waite who were held captive but managed to derive great joy when they were moved from airless cells to one where a portion of sky was visible. Where did they get their sense of peace?

Now think of basically unhappy people who seem to have most of life's goodies. They may have health, wealth, and freedom so try to work out where their dissatisfaction comes from. Listen to their complaints. Remember events that should have made you happy but did not. Now try to be grateful for the things you did today. It is impossible to be grateful and unhappy.

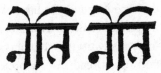

MARY MAGDALENE IN THE GARDEN
(ST JOHN'S GOSPEL 20:11–18)

Quieten yourself in the usual way and become aware of any sounds you can hear outside the room. After a little time, allow your attention to come inwards and note what sounds you can hear within the room. Finally, draw your attention further inwards and see if you can notice any sounds within yourself. You may be able to hear the sound of air as it come quietly through your nostrils. Note your breathing for this will help you to attain silence. God's revealing word is often best received in silence. Now begin the meditation.

Imagine Mary Magdalene in the garden on the morning of the resurrection. Jesus is alive now only in her memory. Otherwise He is dead and she is inconsolable. Then He appears but she is so close to Him that she does not recognise Him. She cannot believe that He would come to her. Could this be the same for you and I? Has Jesus tried to be an active presence for us during these last months without our being aware of it? As Jesus has said to us through the prophet Jeremiah, 'When you seek me you shall find me, when you seek me with all your heart, I will let you find me – it is Yahweh who speaks' (Jer 29: 13–14). Try to be open to Christ's word in your heart for some time and then close the meditation.

THE TOWEL MEDITATION

Use one of the usual preparatory exercises.

Imagine you are holding a towel in your hands. It's an attractive towel with a nice colour and design. Think of its life history. Most of the time it spends its life neatly folded, stored away, tidy, warm, clean and safe, but it is not much use to anyone. The towel is only really useful when it is taken out into the cold world, opened up, spread out, wrapped around somebody. The person is probably uncomfortable due to being wet. The towel absorbs all the wet and makes no fuss about it.

The person who used the towel to soak up all the wet is not necessarily grateful. In all likelihood the towel is left in a heap on the floor where it gets dirty and trodden upon. Next comes the turmoil of the washing machine where the towel is tumbled around and twisted and gets knotted up. Think of the movement, the noise, the commotion it has to endure. Finally, after much turbulence, it finds itself out in the sun. It is stretched out to its fullest extent. Finally it does not feel used, abused or slighted. It has obtained its reward. It can begin to fly in the fresh breeze and bask in the warmth and radiance of the sun. It is just being.

That is what the towel really likes. That is what makes life worthwhile.

Now go over the story again, but this time you 'become' the towel. Think of the times you felt used, damaged, put upon. Also consider the occasions when you felt people threw you aside, never thinking of your feelings, because they had no further use for you. Now see if you can recall a time of cleansing in your life. A time when you basked in the sun and found your true worth again. Give thanks to God for such a time. Stay there for as long as you can ... do you feel better now?

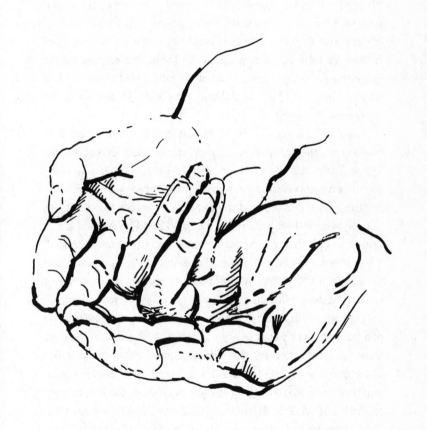

OUR FAITH HISTORY LINE

Know Thyself.

INSCRIPTION, TEMPLE OF APOLLO, DELPHI

Fr Tony de Mello occasionally advised a reflective backward gaze over our lives to see if such an action could teach us anything about the way that God has been active in our personal history. Fr John English, a Canadian Jesuit, recommended the same thing. He has devised what he calls a 'faith history' line and you might find it useful. Many people do. How do you undertake such a project?

The idea, basically, is to let our minds wander back in prayer over the years of our infancy, youth, adolescence, middle age and later life. We try to look at events or people who may have been signposts to God for us during those periods. So during the prayer periods I let my mind settle on certain events, or people, who influenced me for the good and I try to see God at work through their actions in the situations I am praying about. If this gives me a clearer comprehension of God's presence and activity in my life I offer gratefulness to the person or moment when that deep realisation of God's goodness dawned for me.

The idea is that you draw a horizontal line across the middle of a large sheet of paper as shown in the illustration on the next page. You then tick off the different time zones of your life along that line. Above that mark you note down an event from that time zone that seems significant, and below the line you try to work out what faith meaning that event may have for you. As you are trying to find out where the finger of God was active in your life during this phase, you bring to mind people or events which may have been bringers of God to you. For example, you might mark down at the beginning of the line the earliest infancy memory you have. Your next mark might be for an event in your childhood, another during your adolescence, another for mid-life, and yet another for senior years – if you have got that far. Each of these marks represents a particular time in your life.

To give this experience fuller meaning, it is suggested that you take a relevant passage of scripture to help deepen the prayer exercise, and I have selected possible gospel passages which you might use when doing this exercise for yourself. In essence then, what we are trying to do here is get in touch with the story of God's action in your life for, if we believe that God is constantly trying to communicate with us, we may also wish to seek clarification about where this communication has occurred and what meaning it might have for us.

This then is why I might like to reflect on various stages of my life and if events or persons come to mind during my prayerful reflecting, I simply stay with the image or scene which has come to mind before giving thanks for those who made it possible.

The event

INFANCY	CHILDHOOD	YOUTH	ADOLESCENCE	MID-LIFE	SENIOR YEARS
Being lost on the sea shore	Being told stories about Jesus as a youth	Extended family nourished me	Being brought to the country-side	Reflecting on people who have given me life	Think of an event
Psalm 139	*Luke 2:39–40*	*Luke 2:25–32*	*Luke 2:51–52*	*Luke 4: 16–30*	

Faith Meaning

God looking after me even at an early age	A positive image of God developing in me	Goodness of God shown to me	Seeing God in the beauty of nature	Seeing those individuals as God's gift to me for innovation	Did God grace me through the event

I have been using this exercise myself during the past few months whilst I worked with reflection groups in Africa and they found the activity a fascinating and powerful one. In order to explain to them how the 'faith history' line works I reflected on my own faith chronology and related incidents from that story so that they could do the same for themselves. They found it easiest to lay out a large sheet of white paper on the ground and on it they drew a long diagonal line through the centre. They then marked in the notable events of their lives in something like the manner described below.

THE EVENT
(Outline the Event)
___ Infancy
___ Childhood
___ Youth
___ Adolescence
___ Mid-life
___ Senior years

THE MEANING
(What meaning does this event have for me in my faith life?)

Event One. Infancy
As I cast my mind back to my very earliest pre-childhood memories, one abiding picture stands out with me. I was about three years of age at the time and had been out with my family on holidays on a rocky Irish beach. According to reports I somehow managed to stray away from my family group and the absence was noted some little time later. A great lorry with a loudspeaker on the back began to motor along the beach announcing to all who were present that a small boy who pronounced his name as 'Sony' had been found and was now being entertained up in the local convent. When my mother finally located me I was sitting up on a sideboard in the convent being fed chocolate by some of the local nuns. Apparently I looked quite pleased with myself. As I reflect on that incident now, what I am struck by is that even at that early stage it seems to me that

God may have been at work looking after me. As part of my faith history I might reflect and pray about this and take a passage such as Psalm 139 (verses 13–14). The meaning for me is that God has looked after me from the beginning and continues to look after me, even up to the present day.

Event Two. Childhood
Here one again tries to see where God may have been present in one's history. I choose an event from my childhood and try to see if it has a faith meaning for me now in retrospect. I may also choose a passage of scripture to see if this can cast further light on the meaning of the event. The scene that came to my mind whilst I reflected on my earlier life was a picture of evenings spent together at home in my childhood, where some of my brothers and sisters would sit around my father's arm-chair while he took up a book of stories which were centred around the youthful Christ. I can still see the illustrations in the book depicting a youthful and energetic boy Jesus. As I think and pray about this scene I become conscious of the way images of God are developed by each one of us and I am particularly conscious of how grateful I am that the first images of God I was given were ones of a loving, youthful and attractive figure. I know from subsequent work with people that such an image of God is by no means universal and is not one that all others have enjoyed. I could have been handed down an image of a harsh and unrelenting God which might well have permanently affected the way I see and think about the Creator, so in this section I reflect in prayer on Luke 2:39–40 and give thanks that the image I was given was a helpful one and not a hindrance to my future faith growth. All of us are dependent on others for the type of image we have of God. I give thanks for the image I was handed down in my childhood and for those who gave it to me.

Event Three. Youth

As I pray over this phase of my life a picture comes clearly to mind. I recall my granny who as an old lady, in my memory anyway, always seemed to wear large, dumpy, black dresses and had a fine purple ornament pinned to her bosom. In my early school years I visited her home during lunch hour each day as she resided quite close to my school. I remember her as being kind, sitting in a large armchair after lunch each day with a tin of her favourite sweets beside her. They rapidly became my favourite sweets too as she never failed to keep me constantly supplied. When I think over this scene, I am struck by a sense of the extended family and have been inspired by a sense of goodness of those around me. I might recall a gospel passage such as Luke 2:25–32, where Simeon waits patiently for a glimpse of the Lord. I am struck by how easily I was given a glance at the Lord by the goodness and kindness of my grandmother.

Event Four. Adolescence

When a Jew was asked in olden times, 'Who is your God?' he would always answer, 'God is the one who' and he would begin to relate events and deeds which God performed with His people. God's actions in the world were the thing that mattered to him. As we go through this prayer exercise, we try to see how Christ might have been interacting with us. As you reflect over your adolescent years, you may be struck by an event or an individual who was, in a sense, Christ for you. You must choose your own figure or event but I recall one Jesuit scholastic who spent his weekends unselfishly taking a group of us students away on rural outings. In my memory, which is probably flawed, I recall this young Jesuit bringing groups of us to the mountains, sea and lakes around Dublin and during those early years I think I developed a sense of God's beauty showing itself to me in nature. This is the gift I was given. Perhaps the Lord, during that time, found it easiest to show His goodness in the changing beauty of the seasons that surrounded us. In the gospel passage I choose here, Luke 2:51–52, I call to mind Jesus in His youth when He led a hidden life with His parents and increased in wisdom and in stature thanks to the care and love lavished on Him by His parents.

Event Five. Young Adulthood
Again here you choose an event or series of events where God seemed to be particularly present in your life. For me the picture that immediately comes to mind is of my earliest years training to be a Jesuit, straight after school, when I spent my time with a group of other young men deciding whether God was calling us to be Jesuits. The establishment we lived in was spartan and the time-table that we adhered to can only be described as relentless, but the energy and enthusiasm of my companions helped in no small way to make the experience a worthwhile one and to sharpen the focus of the decision I had to make. So here I mull over the gifts of choice which were presented to me and I particularly give thanks for those who shared the road with me. Selecting a gospel passage for this period of my life, I have chosen Matthew 3:13–17, where Jesus Himself is in an extremely eventful phase of His life and is supported greatly by the friendship of John the Baptist in the difficult decisions he had to make.

Event Six. Mid-life
Once again in the 'faith history' line you are invited at this point to recall events or persons in your life who are or were important to you during your middle years. This will allow you to see more clearly how and where God may have been active for you. As I recall in prayer this time in my life, I am particularly

struck by the people of vision and openness that I was lucky enough to encounter. I am also struck by God's ability to be present or show Himself in moments of crisis or pain in my life. I recall some events which shed light on this and you are invited to do the same. It was during this phase in my life that I first encountered Tony de Mello as well as a number of others of similar ilk whose attitude to life and vision of God has profoundly affected me. De Mello, as did the other notable figures in my life at this stage, strongly believed that events which may be either for good or evil are constantly happening to us. In particular Tony de Mello stressed that we ourselves are the ones who choose to appropriate 'life' or 'death' traits out of these situations. He stressed that one should not worry too much whether the travels and paths one chooses bring delights or troubles. The important thing is to travel. Just go. It seems to me now that many people remain in a rut for much of their lives. They do the opposite of what De Mello recommends. They choose not to move at all rather than take a risk. Like the character Molloch, in Milton's *Paradise Lost*, they decide that rather than be less, they would prefer not to be at all. I try to see if this has a faith meaning for me in my life. I choose a gospel passage to see if this can cast further meaning on the event. The scene that comes to mind here is Christ's own self-discovery of His gifts as related in Luke 4:16–30. I ruminate upon my successes and failures and give thanks for the areas of my life where I found fulfilment. I also ponder over the rhythm of work and relaxation within my life and try to discover if the two elements are in harmony.

Event Seven. Recent Years

Again here I choose a passage of scripture, perhaps a psalm, which might help me enter a process of contemplation and reflection whereby I can meet God directly and come to understand how He has been engaging with me in my own life situations. Perhaps Psalm 105 might be suitable here: 'Seek the Lord and His strength, seek His presence continually'. We endeavour to comprehend that we are made by and for God. When we move in His direction we are on the right wavelength, like pigeons coming home to roost. When our life moves in the wrong direction we feel confused and out of focus almost as if we were going the wrong way down a motorway. On such occasions we need to be alert to 'go back' signs, or periods of desolation, for these are trying to tell us something. Attempt to be like St Ignatius of Loyola who had the ability to listen attentively and carefully to an inner presence deep within his being. He was a perpetually sensitive listener to the word of God.

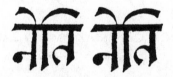

THE TALENTS
(MATTHEW 25:14–30)

Try to remember that when you are tensed, worked-up, keyed-up or knotted-up your body realises it and puts your blood pressure up. Your breathing becomes irregular and your whole physical, mental and emotional being suffers. You need to wind down, calm down and settle down in order to relax and ponder over what the Lord may be trying to say to you.

First read the gospel story and prepare yourself for prayer. Then begin, thinking about the three characters in the story who were given talents. Look at the different ways in which they used those gifts. After some time, allow your imagination to place you in the gospel scene. What talents do you think you have been given by God? How have you used them? Were you generous or mean in their use? Some people don't recognise their own talents. The character who was cursed in the story was not the one who had tried and failed but the one who had been too fearful to risk using his talents in the first place. Try to say to yourself, 'I'd rather have tried and failed than not to have tried at all'. Some people have a great gift of developing the gifts of others. Have I drawn out the talents of those around me during the past months? If I have, I give thanks for that fact. If I have not, I ask that I may be a greater giver of encouragement in the future.

'YOU CAN MAKE ME CLEAN'
(LUKE 5:12–16)

Lord Jesus Christ, we come to you in meditation to discover who we are and the possibilities you open up before us. Help us see ourselves with Your eyes, as You Yourself see us. Bestow on us strength and hope for the next step of our journey.

First read the story from St Luke's Gospel.

Settle yourself and become quiet. Use one of the preparatory exercises. In the quietness of your heart, picture yourself visiting your doctor's office where you are going for a check-up as you have not been feeling well recently. In imagination, sit in the doctor's office and watch and listen to the doctor as he tells you the results of your medical tests. You are not well. In fact you may not have long to live. The doctor encourages you to take note of this. Now be quiet within yourself and try to gauge your feelings as you take in the news you have just been given.

What feelings arise within you?

Where do you want to go as you leave the doctor's office?

Whom do you want to break the news to first?

As you break the news to your friends, what is their response?

Do you hear them talking about you?

If so, what kind of things are they saying about you?

Do you feel the news you have received will change the way you will live the rest of your life?

Take a few minutes with Jesus and share your feelings with Him.

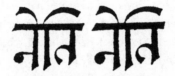

THE INFIRM WOMAN
(LUKE 13:10–17)

First read the scripture passage.

Then begin by relaxing and settling down. Try to sit up fairly straight, resting your hands in front of you on your lap. Uncross your legs and place your feet flat on the floor. Just take a few moments to settle down in this position. You might feel more comfortable if you close your eyes but leave them a little open if you prefer. Find out what feels right and comfortable for you. Now begin to take slow and deep breaths and gently let them go with a full sigh. Continue with these slow and deep breaths for a couple of minutes. Imagine these breaths as they come through your nostrils to the back of your throat, down to your shoulders and into your chest area. Follow the breath in your imagination as it circles around your backbone and makes its way right down to your belly-button. Relax as you breathe out and let the breath flow freely. Your awareness is now focused on your natural breathing. Allow each breath to enter and depart quietly at its own pace. Concentrate at the beginning on following the flow of your breath as it comes in through your nostrils, then settles, and slowly is exhaled through your mouth.

Think about the poor woman and her plight. She had a spirit of infirmity for eighteen years and was bent over and could not straighten herself. Think of her view and her vision. All she could see each day was the little patch directly in front of her. She must have felt like a blinkered horse. She could hardly see beyond her nose. At least she knew it. Think of the times we have been blinkered in our views and our behaviour too. How we were very short-sighted in our actions. Now consider how the Lord, without being asked, changed the poor woman's vista and life. Perhaps He will do the same for me if I ask Him. When you are finished the meditation, thank the Lord for the time you have both spent together.

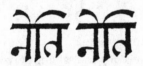

THE BACK-PACK

This fantasy exercise can be helpful in a school environment as the students make their way into one of their final exam years.

Close your eyes and begin to take slow and deep breaths gaining a sense that your breathing is slowing down. Now just imagine that you are breathing in warmth and relaxation. It may help if you tell yourself you are seeking calmness in your life as you breathe in and that you are hoping to dispel tension as you breathe out. Just relax and let go. If you are undertaking this fantasy exercise in a school environment or in a room with other people, you may hear some of your neighbours shuffling or moving around. You may even hear coughing or loud human voices but you try not to let this interfere with what you are doing right now. During the fantasy exercise, you invoke as many senses as possible. These may be a powerful stimulus both to induce relaxation and to generate imagery. In your imagination, make use of sight, sounds, smells, taste, temperature, touch and internal sensations.

Now begin. Take a few deep breaths and allow your body to relax. In your imagination, picture yourself on a journey in the countryside. You are carrying a heavy back-pack. Note the scenery as you pass through it and become aware of sights and sounds as they intrude on your senses. You may hear bird-song or cattle lowing. You may even become aware of the smell of new-mown hay. After a while you become conscious of the weight of the pack on your back. Build up the feeling that it contains all the anxieties and disquiets of your life at present. Now take the pack off and place it on the ground and rest awhile. Open your pack carefully and take out the contents one by one. Examine each item carefully and see what feelings it brings to mind. Now return each object to the pack and bind the whole lot up securely. Find a safe place to hide away the back-pack for you will be continuing your journey without it. Have a sense that you can always go back and reclaim the back-pack if you want to. How does it feel now to travel without the heavy load? Just be aware of the sensation of lightness and carefreeness. See if you can hold on to that feeling as you come back to the present place.

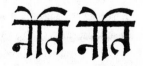

CONVERSATION WITH JESUS

Use a starter exercise.

Now begin the conversation. Taking on certain roles in a fantasy, like playing the part of a friend walking along the beach, provides a safe way for us to get in touch with thoughts and feelings that otherwise might remain unexpressed. The pain of parting is softened by offering the possibility of meeting again. This is a standard procedure to bring people gently out of a meditation or fantasy exercise. It is important to do this slowly and sensitively so that the change between different states of consciousness is not too abrupt. The silence, following a scripted fantasy, can often be deafening and there is no need to rush the group into activity. Allow the silence to reap its own reward.

Processing the fantasy. If you are doing this meditation in a group you may find it helpful to process the material afterwards by giving each participant a sheet of paper and a pencil on which they can write down what happened for them, or the participants might like to share what went on for them with a partner in the group. Listening to your partner is a skill which needs practice. Deciding whether the group members will benefit from paired sharing is also a matter of judgement. Sometimes group members find it very helpful. At other times they would find it an intrusion. Some participants may have delved into material too personal to share. In a school situation some participants find this form of prayer very threatening and I try to provide a convenient space before the session where a reluctant student can opt out of participating. Whilst I normally recommend closing the eyes during the exercise, some people find this difficult to do. It somehow signals a loss of control and therefore becomes an anxiety-provoking experience. It is certainly not helpful to force the issue and insist that the students close their eyes. Only by going through the fantasy will they be able to trust that the experience is a safe one. You might tell those who find the eye-closing instruction a difficult one but who are anxious to conform to your request that they can open their eyes now and again if they so wish. This allows them to stay fairly focused.

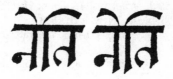

BIBLIOGRAPHY

de Mello, SJ, Anthony, *Sadhana – a Way to God*, Gujarat Sahitya
	Prakash, Anand, India, 1978.
– *The Song of the Bird*, Gujarat Sahitya Prakash, Anand, India, 1987.
– *The Prayer of the Frog*, Gujarat Sahitya Prakash, Anand, India, 1988.
– *One Minute Wisdom*, Gujarat Sahitya Prakash, Anand, India, 1985.
– *The Heart of the Enlightened*, Collins, Fount Paperbacks, 1989.
– *Taking Flight*, Doubleday, New York, 1988.
– *Contact with God – Retreat Conferences*, Gujarat Sahitya Prakash,
	Anand, India, 1990.
– *Call to Love*, Gujarat Sahitya Prakash, Anand, India, 1991.

There are three videos by Fr Tony de Mello, SJ, available.
– *Wake Up, Spirituality for Today*, With Tony de Mello, SJ, Tabor
	Publishing.
– *A Way to God for To-Day*, Tabor Publishing,
– *Re-discovery of Life*, Available from Veritas, Dublin.

Audio Cassette Tapes.
Sadhana (12 Tapes)
Wake Up To Life (12 Tapes)
Wellsprings (8 Tapes)
De Mello *Satellite Retreat* (4 Tapes)
Issued by the We and God Spirituality Centre, Fusz Memorial, St
	Louis University, 3601 Lindell Blvd., St Louis, MO 63108.

Abhishiktananda, *Prayer*, SPCK, London, 1972
Baldwin, Sr Joanna, CSA, *Learning about Retreats*, Mowbray, London,
	1982.
Barry, William A., SJ, and Connolly, William J., SJ, *The Practice of
	Spiritual Direction*, The Seabury Press, New York, 1982.
Barry, William A., SJ, *Paying attention to God: Discernment in Prayer*,
	Ave Maria Press, Notre Dame, Indiana: 1990; *Finding God in
	All Things: A Companion to the Spiritual Exercises*, Ave Maria
	Press, Notre Dame, Indiana, 1991.
Carroll, Susan, *Group Exercises for Adolescents*, Sage, London, 1993.
Church, Connie, *Crystal Love*, Villard Books, New York, 1988.
Cooke, Grace, *Meditation*, The White Eagle Publishing Trust, England,
	1955.

Covey, Stephen R., *The 7 Habits of Highly Effective People*, Simon & Schuster, New York, 1989.

Cummins, Norbert, OCD, *Freedom to Rejoice*, Harper Collins, London, 1991.

Davis, Roy Eugene, *An Easy Guide to Meditation*, Mercier Press, Cork, 1988.

Donze, Mary Terese, ASC, *In My Heart Room*, Liguori Publications, USA, 1982.

Downing, G., *The Massage Book*, Penguin, Harmondsworth, 1982 edition.

Fontana, David Dr, *The Meditator's Handbook*, Element Books, Dorset, 1992

Fontana, David, *The Elements of Meditation*, Element Books, Dorset, 1991.

Freeman, Laurence, OSB, *Light Within*, Darton Longman and Todd, London, 1986.

Garfield, Patrica, *The Healing Power of Dreams*, Simon and Schuster, NewYork, 1992.

Green, S.J., Thomas H., *Weeds Among the Wheat: Discernment – where Prayer and Action Meet*, Ave Maria Press, Notre Dame, Indiana, 1984.

Hamilton-Merritt, Jane, *A Meditator's Diary*, Unwin Paperbacks, London, 1976.

Hart, William, *Vipassana Meditation*, Harper, San Francisco, 1987.

Hay, Louise L, *You can heal your life*, London, 1988.

Hebblethwaite, Margaret, *Finding God in All Things: Praying with St. Ignatius*, Collins, Fount Paperbacks, London, 1987.

Hughes, Gerard W., *Oh God, Why? .... Direction in Prayer*, The Bible Reading Fellowship, England, 1993.

Hughes, Gerard, SJ, *God of Surprises*, Longman and Todd, London, 1986.

Johnston, William, *Being In Love*, Collins, Fount Paperbacks, London, 1989.

Johnson, William, *The Inner Eye of Love*, Harper & Row, San Francisco 1978.

Kabat-Zinn, Jon, *Mindfullness Meditation for Everyday*, Piatkus, 1994.

Kamalashila, *Sitting, A Guide to Good Meditation Posture*, Windhorse Publications, Glasgow, 1988.

Le Shan, Lawrence, *How to Meditate*, Turnstone Press Ltd, Wellingborough, 1983.

Levine, Stephen, *Guided Meditation (Explorations and Healings)*, Gateway Books, Bath 1991.

Lonsdale, David, SJ, *Eyes to see, Ears to Hear: An Introduction to Ignatian – Spirituality*, Darton Longman and Todd, London, 1990.

Marlin, Brigid, *From East to West*, Collins, Fount Paperbacks, London, 1989.

Maryland Province of the Society of Jesus, *Place Me With Your Son: The Spiritual Exercises in Everyday Life*, Maryland, 1985.

Murgatroyd, Stephen, *Counselling and Helping*, Routledge, London, 1985.

Nash, Wanda, *At Ease with Stress*, Darton Longman and Todd, 1988,

Nash, Wanda, Newbook 9, *People need Stillness*, Darton Longman and Todd Ltd, London, 1992.

Novak, John (Jyotish), *How to Meditate*, Crystal Clarity Publishers, USA, 1989.

Pennington, M. Basil, OCSO, *Centering Prayer*, An Image Book, Doubleday, New York, 1982.

Puhl, Louis J., SJ, *The Spiritual Exercises of St. Ignatius based on Studies in the Language of the Autograph*, Loyola University Press, Chicago 1951.

Valles, Carlos, SJ, *Unencumbered by Baggage*, Gujarat Sahaitya Prakash, Anand, India, 1988.

Vandana, Sister, *Waters of Fire*, Asian Trading Corporation, Bangalore 1989.

Weitzmann, Kurt, *et. al.*, *The Icon*, Bracken Books, London, 1982.

West, Serene, *Very Practical Meditation*, Whitford Press, Pennsylvania 1981.

Wilson, Jim, *First Steps in Meditation for Young People*, James Clarke & Como Ltd., London, 1957.

Wilson, Paul, *The Calm Technique*, Thorsons, London, 1987.

Zanzig, Thomas, *Learning to Meditate*, St Mary's Press, Christian Brothers Publications, Winona, Minnesota, 1990.